FROM THE JAWS OF THE DRAGON

Sales Tales and Other Marginally Related Stuff

From Sales Satirist

Richard Plinke

Dedication

This book is dedicated to Bill Zifcheck. When I was starting out with little experience, no contacts or street cred, and trying to make my way in New York City, most of the big-time buyers wouldn't give me the time of day. Bill, on the other hand, would not only share his time whenever I called, but would spend hours giving me advice and helpful tips. Bill taught me you don't have to be the painful possibility of a rose thorn to be successful.

When I started in sales...

What I didn't know was, once I got through all the misconceptions, blind alleys and unrealistic expectations, I was embarking on the adventure of a lifetime, and I've spent a lifetime, 35 years, dancing in the jaws of the dragon and loving every minute of it.

From *How to Sell the Plague*

Published in *Sales & Marketing Management,* February 2011

Courage

The quality of mind or spirit that enables a person to face difficulty, danger or pain.

Inaction breeds doubt and fear. Action breeds confidence and courage. If you want to conquer fear, do not sit home and think about it. Go out and get busy.

Dale Carnegie

Success is not final; failure is not fatal: it is the courage to continue that counts.

Winston Churchill

Courage doesn't always roar. Sometimes courage is the little voice at the end of the day that says, "I will try again tomorrow."

Mary Anne Radmacher

Richard Plinke

You will never do anything in this world without courage. It is the greatest quality of the mind, next to honor.

Aristotle

Courage! What makes a King out of a slave?
Courage! What makes the flag on the mast to wave?
Courage! What makes the elephant charge his tusk, in the misty mist or the dusky dusk?
What makes the muskrat guard his musk?
Courage! What makes the sphinx the seventh wonder?
Courage! What makes the dawn come up like thunder?
Courage! What makes the Hottentot so hot? What puts the "ape" in apricot?
What have they got that I ain't got?
Courage!

Cowardly Lion from *The Wizard of Oz*

Contents

What You See Is What You Get

It is said that a shoe company decided to open up a new market in an emerging third world country just starting to develop a viable economy, so they sent two salespeople in to cultivate the area.

After a couple days, the company received two separate messages, one from each of their sales reps. The first was, "I'm returning on the next flight. I can't sell these people anything. Nobody here wears shoes!"

The second message read, "What a great market. The prospects are unlimited. Nobody here wears shoes!"

Introduction

I came across this employment ad on the Internet:

Vice President, Strategic Accounts - a senior role focused on structuring and selling large "front office" legal outsourcing engagements to the legal departments of large corporations. This position is focused on migrating the current sales model from transactional outsourcing projects to large multi-year, multi-FTE (full time equivalent). This person will be focused on deeply penetrating a small number of accounts.

Wrong. This person will be focused on deeply penetrating WTF!

Albert Einstein said, "Any intelligent fool can make things bigger and more complex. It takes a touch of genius, and a lot of courage to move in the opposite direction." Well, I'm not sure I have much genius or true courage, but I know bovine excrement when I see it, and that's mostly what I write about in this book.

I know a great deal about bovine excrement because I've been in sales for over 35 years. In that time, I've been a salesman, a sales manager, and a sales trainer, and I've owned a few sales-focused businesses. So when Frank Sinatra sang, "I've been a puppet, a pauper, a pirate, a poet, a pawn and a king. I've been up and down and over and out and I know one thing. Each time I find myself flat on my face, I pick myself up and get back in the race," I have some idea from where he speaks.

That's life.

That's sales.

Welcome aboard.

This book is not your father's Oldsmobile when it comes to sales. To be perfectly honest, I'm not a big fan of most traditional books on sales. Most of them are comprised mainly of derivative material or gimmicky methodologies developed for the sole purpose of transporting money from your pocket to the pocket of the newest sham-shaman here to set you free. A lot of it reminds me of an Eastern mystic I ran into in Colorado in 1971. A friend of mine who was looking for the truth (like you were going to find that in Colorado in 1971 where you couldn't turn over a rock without unearthing another misguided seeker of meaning) dragged me to a meeting in the mountains to see the boy prophet from the mysterious and spiritual land of Bharatvarsh.

What a hoot the night turned out to be. After sitting through the show of flowing robes, large feather fans, burning incense, eerie sitar music and more disingenuous oratory than you'll find at a political debate, the latest-with-the-greatest finally showed, said about ten words, and disappeared behind layers of orange and white satin-like sheets that made up the sides of the opulent tent that was both festive and solemn at the same time.

And then they set the hook. For only ten bucks, you could go into a small adjoining tent for a brief and private audience with the holy one, where enlightenment was assured.

I couldn't resist.

I sat in front of a guy who looked somewhere between 15 and 45 years old. He kept his head bowed and never looked me in the eye. He said a few things in a tongue I didn't recognize (like the gibberish from the Andy Kaufman character Latka on the TV series *Taxi*), and then he told me to close my eyes. He put his thumb and index finger on my eyelids and gently pressed against them.

"Do you see the white light?" he asked.

Of course I did. Everyone sees a white light when they press their fingers against their closed eyelids.

"The white light is the light of knowledge," he said.

"Congratulations." I was immediately whisked out of the tent by a couple of Gunga Din-era thugs straight from Central Casting and introduced to a recruiter who gave me the full pitch. Apparently, gaining enlightenment was as easy as giving them most of my money, on a recurring basis.

A small price to pay for ultimate wisdom and the essential secrets of the universe.

Tony Robbins, the motivational guru extraordinaire who teaches people to give him money, said, "Success is doing what you want to do, when you want, where you want, with whom you want, as much as you want."

Really?

I thought that was narcissism.

Maybe that's the way it works when you live on your own South Pacific island and fly around the world in a private jet, but if you plan to be successful in sales, you'd better learn to do what's best for your client and subjugate your own wants for a later time (perhaps when you, too, live on your own island, and only $2,595 to get started).

This book is not about that kind of stuff, but please feel free to send me your money, if you're so disposed.

What you are about to read is a collection of blogs, articles and essays I've written. They are ostensibly about the field of sales, but since I see selling as a great metaphor for life, they tend to drift and weave a bit, so bear with me. Every story I tell is true (as much as anything is true), and they all happened to me, except the ones that didn't (which I identify).

I hope you enjoy reading them as much as I enjoyed writing them. Before you begin, however, please allow me one more fractured, overwrought metaphor. (I can't resist, especially the Herman Melville quote from *Moby Dick*.)

Sales is like a water pie. "Whenever I find myself growing grim about the mouth; whenever it is a damp, drizzly November in my soul; whenever I find myself involuntarily pausing before coffin warehouses, and bringing up the rear of every funeral I meet; and especially whenever my hypos get such an upper hand of me that it requires a strong moral principle to prevent me from deliberately stepping into the street, and methodically knocking people's hats off," I take a slice of water pie. Water pie is the stuff of dreams and possibilities, and it's a constant reminder of what this is all about: helping other people. That makes all the bovine excrement worth it.

Every time you take a slice of water pie, the void you leave fills in immediately with the hopes and aspirations of all your brethren, picking up the tab. As for all those seemingly debilitating storms we go through periodically, they simply replenish the pie with fresh, clean water.

And the best thing about water pie is that it tastes like anything you want it to taste like. Just use your creativity and believe.

It's all up to you.

Allentown, Pennsylvania
October 21, 2012

Prologue

So you want to be a sales puke.

Me? I never wanted to be in sales and only ended up here by dumb luck. The thought of all those hucksters and liars as depicted in the media and entertainment was enough to scare me away. But apparently providence is stronger than the discord, disillusionment and lack of ethics portrayed by characters like Willie Loman from *Death of a Salesman* or Professor Harold Hill in *The Music Man*, and finally, after being baited, switched and hooked (like in any good con game), I jumped at the chance to sell my soul to the devil. And 35-plus years later, here I am, still prepping and schlepping and still chasing those elusive sales.

Ah, those elusive sales, the stuff of imagination that spawned the modern marketing industry, wherein the art of selling safely resides and flourishes under the simple belief that is predicated on the principle that no truth is sacred and any idea or notion can be spun into any other idea or notion with the right positioning. No, not lies—

positioning—a euphemism of sometimes hilarious proportion that has given us delightfully original misuse of language, all in the good name of moving product.

Like a local bank in my hometown. They ran an ad warning customers to be wary of other banks, with the line "Did your bank sell you down the river?" In the printed ad there was a depiction of a frightened man in a wooden rowboat about to go over a large waterfall. Printed on the side of the boat was the name "S.S. Hugo First." The copy read, "Want this to be the last time a local bank sells out and leaves you in uncharted waters?" In these times of large banks gobbling up smaller banks as quickly as they can until they are no longer profitable and are forced to sell out to even bigger banks on their way to unprofitability, it was a likable ad with a valuable message and I imagine it worked well for them.

The only problem is that it was sophistry of the highest order. You see, many of the folks involved in that bank were involved in another local bank a few years ago that did exactly what they were warning against: they sold out to a bigger bank, leaving their former customers in extremely turbulent waters. I know; I was one of those customers who got caught plunging down a raging river with no paddle. In spite of that, I have to admit it takes real *chutzpah* to roll out an advertising campaign that warns people about somebody else doing something painful to them that you've already done to them (and may very well do to them again in the future). Although the ad may be disingenuous to an extent, the bottom line is that it's smart marketing.

Almost as smart as a candy bar company that wanted to introduce a new size for their popular candy bars a few decades ago when marketing was just starting to catch on to its real power of persuasion. The candy bars in question had been around a very long time and had been the same size since the inception of the company, way back when people went into business because they wanted to produce a quality product. However, as profitability replaced product as the main impetus for showing up in the morning to grind cocoa beans and mix the brown, powdered gold with overly processed sugar, some bean-counter (literally) decided the company was being way too generous with their delightful concoctions and reduced the size of the candy bars.

Which brought up an interesting sales dilemma: How do you sell a smaller candy bar to the chocolate-consuming public for the same price without harming the brand? Out of the swirling vortex of creation came inspiration from a crackerjack marketeer who had a brilliant idea—they would package the candy bars in new, brightly colored wrappers and in big, bold print, they would add the words "New Size!"

As absurd as it sounds, it worked. Sales actually increased with the introduction of the new merchandizing scheme for the smaller candy bars at the same price, which says a lot about us and helps explain how a few shifty but well-packaged rascals have been elected to positions of authority. As the candy bar company learned, sales really is all about the use of language in positioning a product, a lesson a canning company once used to solve an inventory problem that threatened to send it into bankruptcy.

This story was around before my introduction to the world of business, and has been retold in so many variations and attributed to so many different sources that it's become a kind of mythic fable. I heard it my first week in training, and over the years I've researched it but could never find any substantial information on its origin, only a lot of misinformation and misdirection. It's my favorite sales story, although you could argue it's a marketing story. To me, sales and marketing are pretty much one and the same, the most notable difference being that the salesperson is out on the cold, hard street every day with her smiling face in front of prospects, and, more often than not, leaves with her still-smiling head on a not-so-shiny, rather tarnished and dinged-up, silver-plated platter. Meanwhile, the marketing nerds are back in their safe, warm offices thinking up new ways to get our heads handed to us. It's a swell relationship, but in essence, the same discipline.

It seems that this canning company had purchased a great deal of Russian salmon, but when the fish was canned and distributed, it just sat on the grocery store shelves and didn't sell. It didn't sell because it was white-meat salmon, whereas salmon was by and large pink.

Accordingly, people were put off by the idea of white salmon and afraid to take a risk on something new and different, sadly but usually the case with new and different things. The company had invested a lot of money in the Russian shipment, and as a result, found itself in a precarious cash flow situation. They had to find a way to sell the salmon or risk financial peril.

Finally, some brighter-than-the-average-bear advertising deckhand came up with an idea. They recalled all the salmon, relabeled the cans and shipped them back out. As the story goes, within a few days the entire shipment sold out. What did the new label say that caused the salmon to become so popular? It was a simple but brilliant message that read: "Will not turn pink in the can."

Although the new message on the labels fit the definition of sophistry to a T (cleverly deceptive reasoning), it wasn't a lie; that salmon wouldn't turn pink in a million years, but the implication was that all salmon started out white and turned pink while sitting on the grocer's shelves, and that sounded just a bit too icky for most folks.

Positioning. You can sell almost anything with the right positioning, as these companies found out. And you can position a product to your potential customer much more easily once you've learned how to read and interpret his behavior. Studying human behavior is one of the most enjoyable parts of sales for me. Everybody is unique in one way or another, and trying to figure out what pushes their buttons can be challenging and fun. There are plenty of courses, books and tapes out there that can teach you how to pigeonhole prospects into neatly defined categories, and they're fine, to a point. The problem is that like snowflakes, no two human beings are the same. They can be similar, but never exact copies of each other, so if you want to become good at selling to people, you'd better first learn how to read and understand people.

My entire career has been spent watching and studying human behavior, and it's always fascinating. I've come to realize that people behave in certain ways because they get caught up in who they think they are and who they want to be, and in doing so, lose sight of what it is they're supposed to be accomplishing.

I was at a luncheon recently that was sponsored by a large health insurance company. On the agenda was a workshop on health care in today's business world, with an emphasis on the cost of health insurance. This insurance company insures millions and millions of people, and their business is the business of people's health, or at least it should be.

The affair was a first-rate operation and the room was appointed beautifully with fresh flowers and colorful linen tablecloths. The buffet table was long and elegant, full of food and beverages. There were a few salads and some kind of tuna mix, but the main attraction was roast beef sandwiches on white flour rolls with mayonnaise and other condiments available on the side. They had what looked like homemade potato chips, brownies, chocolate chip cookies, sweetened ice tea and assorted soft drinks. And lots of coffee to wash it all down and give you a little afternoon pick-me-up.

So what's wrong with this picture? The only thing missing on the serving table were shots of whiskey and a few tobacco products. It was the perfect menu for high cholesterol, high blood pressure and high blood sugar; a myriad of heart disease, neurologic disorders and type 2 diabetes accelerators.

I couldn't believe it. What were they thinking? Whose brainchild was the menu and did that person have any clue what the theme of the afternoon was? More fascinating, when I mentioned my observation to the person seated next to me, he looked at me like I had three heads.

I assume I wasn't the only one there who saw the hypocrisy and conflicting messages they were sending with their food choices, but it certainly gave me pause to think about why we're in the midst of a healthcare crisis.

Human behavior can be a powerful elixir of the bizarre and the strange. I was at an airport several years ago, sitting in a hallway next to a bank of pay phones. (Pay phones are old-fashioned cell phones, only they were attached to walls or poles, and you had to put money into a slot to make them work. You couldn't access the Internet with them, but hanging next to the phones on a metal cord was a printed version of the Internet we called the Yellow Pages. Pay phones never lost power and never dropped calls because of a weak signal. Consequently, they were much more reliable and user friendly. And because people used to go out of their houses back then and often traveled to places where there were no pay phones, you sometimes had to actually speak face to face to a fellow human being, using real spoken language. OMG, CYI?)

I was sitting there waiting for my flight to be called and reading a newspaper. A man in a suit and tie and carrying a briefcase was standing next to the phones with a young girl who looked about 4 years old, and who I assumed was his daughter. He was bending over to look her in the eyes and speaking in a tone and vernacular appropriate for a 4-year-old, not baby talk but in clear and animated language that was a bit sing-songy. He was extremely attentive and he appeared to cherish her dearly. He made me feel less than adequate as a father, and I remember experiencing some discomfort; I was threatened by the overt and demonstrative show of affection.

Then the phone rang and he hurried over to pick it up, leaving his daughter looking confused and a bit lost. He immediately launched into a heated discussion with someone who appeared to be his superior about an order that had either been lost or misfiled. As he engaged in the conversation and lost touch with everything else around him, his daughter walked the couple of steps over to him and tugged on his coat.

"Daddy," she said. "I have to go to the bathroom."

He quickly and distractedly looked down and patted her on the head. "Not now, sweetie," he replied.

But she persisted in tugging on his coat and beseeching him to take her to the bathroom, and he continued to be totally preoccupied with his call and pretty much ignored her, occasionally giving her a quick, insincere smile, trying to placate her long enough to take care of the real business at hand. This continued for a while, and eventually she started crying and peed her pants, making a puddle on the floor around her and her daddy's shoes.

What a scene. Here was a guy who appeared to be one thing but turned out to be something completely different, a guy I had admired at first blush, before he exposed his badly misplaced priorities. This guy would tell you and show you he was a great dad, at least when it was convenient. He also didn't listen to what was being said to him, and he didn't process information effectively, a common and debilitating trait in most salespeople. When I played football, we called guys like that "all show and no go."

Studying human behavior is like sailing a boat. You always have to be aware of which way the wind is blowing and always be alert for it to change without warning. And then you have to be able to react quickly and decisively in order to keep sailing ahead smoothly. However, I remember one time being so flummoxed by the behavior of one particular human being that there was no way to react in any constructive manner other than to learn a valuable lesson: Don't believe everything you hear, especially if it's coming from the mouth of another person.

I've spent my career selling advertising, and I was at an advertising convention in Florida where the keynote speaker was a buyer from a large New York advertising agency. This buyer handled a few big accounts and he was responsible for spending *mucho dinero* in media, so I was anxious to hear him speak and hopefully pick up a few valuable tips.

As it turned out, he was mesmerizing. He was witty and charming and a terrific speaker with plenty of interesting anecdotes and funny stories. Since this convention was for media sales reps, the general theme of his presentation was aimed at how to sell advertising to buyers from large New York advertising agencies. He told tale after tale of his encounters with hapless media reps, most of those encounters being of the less-than-successful variety, and he interjected a great deal of advice on how to secure appointments with buyers from large New York advertising agencies. He went on and on about how he wanted fresh, new minds coming to him with fresh, new ideas, and how he wanted them very badly and how he wanted all of us fresh, new reps to keep that in mind as we met with buyers from large New York advertising agencies.

He got me pumped. I couldn't wait to get home and start calling buyers from large New York advertising agencies with all my fresh, new ideas, and I was going to call him first. Well, I made that call, and then a week later I made that call again, and then again, and then again, and on it went until finally after a few months of frustration, I wrote him a letter thanking him for the great advice he'd given me at the convention, and asking him if he ever removed his head from up his ass long enough to take a breath, would he please return my phone call.

So you want to be a sales puke.

Well, strap yourself in tight because it's going to be one hell of a ride.

Would You Buy a Used Car from This Man?

(Note: Citizens Bank is a medium-sized bank with 1,500 branches located in the northeastern part of the United States. They own the naming rights to the stadium where the Philadelphia Phillies play baseball, known as Citizens Bank Park.)

Alexander Hamilton was a real bastard.

Really. He was born in the British West Indies to an unmarried woman, back when it was still a big deal in 1755 or 1757 (depending on which of Hamilton's birth dates you subscribe to).

In today's version of Alexander Hamilton, according to the character portrayed in the Citizens Bank series of TV commercials, he's a great salesman, too.

A bastard salesman.

Aren't we all.

Citizens Bank uses the Hamilton character to help sell their services with the tag line "Good banking is good citizenship." He's a curious choice for a bank trying to position itself as a people-friendly enterprise, and not because he's a bastard. We're much more sophisticated now and have moved on to hating people for wearing the wrong color Air Jordans.

The Hamilton character in the commercials is a kind, caring, grandfatherly type who talks about how a bank ought to treat its customers, from the customer's point of view. It's doubtful Hamilton ever embraced that point of view while he was among the living, based on written history at least. Maybe Citizens Bank knows something the rest of us don't.

There are those who believe Alexander Hamilton's ideas paved the way for a great deal of the economic mess we're in now, while others think he was a genius who created the banking platform used around the world. Regardless of what you believe, few Americans have been as controversial as Hamilton, and in today's banking world where bankers have elevated themselves to the not-so-lofty realm of politicians and shylocks, I would think any type of controversial subject or figure would be wise to avoid. After 2008, banks should be doing more PR to repair their reputations, and although the historically inconsistent Hamilton character is an effective vehicle for trying to achieve just that, it doesn't work for me. As a matter of fact, it has just the opposite effect: it makes me feel like I'm being used.

But that's not my main problem with the ads. I feel much more manipulated by the character himself, rather than the content. The actor who plays Hamilton is Marshal Bell, who was born in September 1942. That makes him 70 years old at present, 21 or 23 years older than Hamilton was when his life was prematurely ended on the future site of now defunct Palisades Park on the New Jersey banks of the Hudson River, where, as Freddy "Boom Boom" Cannon sang about in his 1962 hit (titled "Palisades Park"), I'm sure Hamilton's heart was going "up a like a rocket ship, down a like a roller coaster, fast a like a loop the loop, and a round a like a merry go round" when the hot lead from Aaron Burr's pistol tore into his chest in the most famous duel in American history.

By all accounts, Hamilton was an aggressive, ambitious and somewhat ruthless individual who was steadfast in his beliefs and impatient with those who did not agree with him, not your wise old uncle giving you sound advice and comforting reassurance. Moreover, he was 47 or 49 years old, not 70! It drives me crazy every time I see one of those commercials, and I start yelling at my TV screen like I'm watching another hapless Phillies base runner trying to score from third to home while the other team's catcher is enjoying a beer and a sandwich as he waits for him at the plate.

The first requirement of successful selling is honesty, and honestly, those ads just aren't honest. Unfortunately, most viewers know more about the Kardashians and Snooki than American history, so it's not hard to understand why Citizens Bank thought they could get away with a little whitewashing. But you can't sell your product or service under false pretenses; it never works in the long run.

For a company that has attached its name to one of the coolest places in Philadelphia, you would think they'd know two simple truths: You can't get to heaven on the Frankford El, and you can't fool all the people all the time.

Pretty Packages

Suze Rotolo is dead.

Were you/are you a Dylan fan? I fit more in the "were" category, being in New York shortly after he packed up his tents and moved out of the Greenwich Village scene he might not have invented but certainly molded to his own specific needs. Jimmy O'Flynn, the guy who owned a bar where I worked and his cadre of demented and jaded friends worshipped at the altar of the Great American Troubadour, the Voice of a lost generation. They had been active members of the Knights Templar of early cool, the first scouts of the brigade of imminent change sweeping through the canyons of old New Amsterdam, a buffer of sorts between the Beats and us, and they knew the New York bar scene where early Bob Dylan folklore and the occasional Dylan sighting was the daily currency of the initiated and the hip.

The bar I worked at was called the Black Horse, named in mock tribute to the famous White Horse in The Village (after Jimmy

O'Flynn and company were thrown out one night for lewd and lascivious behavior), where Dylan Thomas was a regular and one night went gently into that good bar and drank himself to death. A few years later, Bob Zimmerman (the real name of the boss progenitor of cryptic, esoteric lyrics) from Minnesota would appropriate the name and go on to become a tremendous influence over the people who influenced me. So I became a huge Dylan fan in my back pages, but not so much today, where he appears to be more a caricature of himself than the most influential singer of the Twentieth Century.

If you are an old-time Dylan fan like me, and if you remember his seminal album *The Freewheelin' Bob Dylan*, then you knew Suze Rotolo. She was the blond on the cover of the album, wrapped around Dylan, as they walked down a Village street in the middle of winter. She was the first hippie chick, the girl every guy wanted to be with and every young woman wanted to look like. She was "it," and we were all smitten from the get-go.

And why, you may ask, is this important to you? Because that album cover was the most impactful packaging of the new order, the beginning of selling product to the want-to-be-there masses. The picture, so real and spontaneous in appearance, was pure Madison Avenue, selling attitude, lifestyle and promises of a new and more meaningful existence. And we were all buying—lock, stock and Volkswagen microbus (extemporaneously sitting in the background, the official vehicle of the Woodstock Generation serendipitously parked next to the most manufactured phenomenon of our time, along with the Beatles, of course—Elvis Presley was a see-Spot-run primer for what these boys would do to the field of music marketing).

That album cover had a huge impact on me and millions of other teenagers crawling out of the "get out of the new (road) if you can't lend your hand" Eisenhower generation and street-racing into the New Frontier, the Kennedy promise of hope and excitement, never once giving any thought or acknowledgement to the obvious contradiction of our simplistic and uninformed opinion that the world did, indeed, suck and was hopeless. After years of safe album art—like the Kingston Trio posed in striped shirts, or the Beach Boys posed in striped shirts, or Buddy Holly and the Crickets not posed in striped shirts but those ridiculous tuxedos like Frank Sinatra and Dean Martin at the Sands—Dylan and Rotolo ushered in a brave new world of mega marketing for the coming music juggernaut with their iconic and freewheeling picture.

And that's my point (finally). Dylan knew how to sell himself. He had to have the goods to deliver when people started buying, but he put himself in a position to sell his product, and the album jacket is a great example of that packaging. Dylan was not only a genius at making relevant, entertaining music, but he was a master at marketing and sales as well. When you boil it down to its pure essence, we're all in the same business, and you can learn from Dylan's example.

Suze Rotolo never traded on her short but meteoric burst of flame across the lower Manhattan sky, but lived most of her life in preferred obscurity. I'm guessing that the short time she spent with Dylan provided enough excitement and pain to last a lifetime. However, before she succumbed to lung cancer, she wrote a book about those amazing days of unharnessed, creative energy. It was titled *A Freewheelin' Time*. In it she talked about how careful Dylan was in choosing his clothing, how he always looked rumpled and thrown together, but not by chance. He wanted to make sure he looked the part, and he was meticulous about it, unlike many salespeople today, whom I will rail against on another occasion.

In the meantime, goodbye Suze Rotolo, the stuff of my early dreams. You did a great job selling me.

Of Deodorants and Dental Floss

If you're in sales, you should read *Confessions of an Advertising Man* by David Ogilvy. It was first published in 1963, back when Kennedy was President, the world had yet to hear the Beatles, and we were still driving our Chevys to the levy. The book was a runaway hit, and has continued to sell well ever since. When I first got into media sales, it was touted as the bible of the advertising industry, and Ogilvy is considered by many to be the father of modern advertising.

So why should you read it? Because advertising is selling. Both fields of endeavor are based on the same principles, with the same expectations—to sell product, and Ogilvy was somewhat monomaniacal when it came to selling product, which is what made me think of him while I was watching the Super Bowl.

Like so many others who seem more engrossed in the commercials than the game itself, my family likes to critique the ads and pick his or her favorites. As they go through this process during the evening, they annotate each opinion (for my benefit) with an obligatory remark like, "I know, it doesn't sell product." Being a disciple of Ogilvy, my question is, if you're not selling product, then what business are you in? A highly visible sector of the advertising community (at least the most highly paid sector) seems to have forgotten that they're in the business of selling, and has come to believe, thanks in large part to Super Bowl exposure, that they are in the entertainment business. David Ogilvy must roll over in his grave every year on Super Bowl Sunday.

This is fairly standard criticism of advertising in general these days, and especially of those ads prepared specifically for a Super Bowl telecast. With that in mind, I decided to conduct my own, very unscientific poll. For a few days after the game, I randomly asked people to name their favorite commercials from the Super Bowl. If they didn't name the advertised product in their identification of the ad, I'd follow up by asking them what product the commercial was advertising. I didn't ask anybody in the advertising or media business since they would be inclined to pay more attention to the ads.

In my research, I questioned 23 people, and two commercials came out ahead. The first was the Bridgestone tire ad featuring a hip beaver practicing a little *quid pro quo*, and the other was the one for the Volkswagen Passat with a young Darth Vader. As it turned out, not one person who named either of those two commercials could tell me what brand was being advertised. They all knew the Darth Vader commercial was for a car, but nobody knew which one, and they guessed the Bridgestone ad was either for a car or a tire, but couldn't remember the brand.

Great entertainment, real bad selling.

Each spot cost $3 million, and, coupled with the enormous production expenses, it was a lot of money to spend with no payback (at least from my unscientific findings). This is most likely the result of neither brand being named until the end of the spots, after the punch line had been delivered and people were preoccupied with savoring the jokes.

On the other hand, many of my respondents named the Snickers commercial with Richard Lewis, and identified it as the "Snickers commercial." (You can find all these spots on YouTube.) That's because the product was part of the joke, not an aside after the fact. Snickers played a prominent role in the gag and the whole delivery depended on the image of a candy bar full of energy providing caffeine and sugar to deliver the message, whereas Bridgestone and Volkswagen were superfluous tags that had nothing to do with the set-up or delivery.

Unfortunately, that's what many salespeople do every day: they try to sell their product without selling their product. The old saw that says you have to sell the sizzle, not the steak, is advice fraught with peril, and if you're not careful, you can sizzle yourself right out of the deal. Sure, you can set up your sales pitch with the sizzle, you can paint pretty pictures for your prospect and dance her around extraneous images and perceptions as you dazzle her with bull-fertilizer (in order to grow the sale, of course), but when it comes time to close, you'd better be offering some genuine features and benefits. As salespeople, our job is to get the prospect to give us money, and the only way to do that is to sell value, real value.

Don't apologize for being in sales and don't apologize for trying to sell. Don't be reluctant to sell your product hard, and don't let people tell you it's no longer fashionable to jump in there selling vigorously and enthusiastically, because that's what we do to make money. Selling is selling and it's as timeless as the guy hawking the latest developments in rock-chiseled wheels along the Tigris and Euphrates rivers as civilization begins its long and arduous crawl to the kickoff of Super Bowl I. We don't get paid to be advisors or consultants or friends; we get paid to sell. If you are more effective being an advisor or a consultant or a friend to accomplish that, have at it, but keep selling.

And read *Confessions of an Advertising Man*; it will make you a better salesperson. If you do, you'll notice something interesting (if you're paying attention). The last two editions I've seen online and in bookstores have brightly colored jackets with white type naming the book and the author. That's called reverse type in the advertising and printing industries because you use white (or light-colored) letters on a dark background instead of printing with dark ink on a light background. In his book, Ogilvy rails against reverse type, saying it doesn't work because it's hard to read and it's the province of hacks.

Talk about irony. Is nobody listening to David Ogilvy anymore? Watching the Super Bowl would certainly lead you to believe that few are, but don't be one of them.

Sell, sell, sell!

Dress for Success

Dress for success? What does that mean anymore? The way many salespeople dress these days, you might think it's a dead concept. I can't believe how I see some sales folk show up for work, as if they put no more thought into their choice of clothes than they did picking a shopping cart at the grocery store: just grab what's handy and go.

Unbelievable.

But then I come from an era when we wore a suit every day, usually a white or Oxford blue shirt, a conservative tie, and shined shoes. Wow, shined shoes—talk about a dead concept! Women wore business suits with skirts, no dresses or pant suits; those would come later in the semi-liberated, post age-of-enlightenment, when women started becoming a more common sight in sales rooms and began asserting their presence, after years of an apologetic posture for having invaded the privileged boys club. Back before President Kennedy made our country a more comfortable and easygoing place, we dressed much more formally all the time. Men even wore suits and ties and hats to ball games, and not the caps you see today, most likely worn backwards or tilted to the side or, worse, one of those flat brim jobs that scream "all the tattoos and body piercings just aren't enough to show you that I have absolutely no idea who I am." Of course, back in those golden, olden days, we were all a bit more uptight and proper in everything we did, which wasn't always a good thing. Some of the relaxing of our social standards has made for a much better, more user-friendly world, but the dress of salespeople shouldn't be one of them.

And I'm not talking about wearing a suit every day (those days are gone forever for most of us), but at least putting some effort into how you look. Not a big deal, you would think, for a professional salesperson.

I was out to lunch one day and a group of Pennsylvania State Police detectives came into the restaurant. They were all wearing conservative suits, white shirts, and stylish, professional ties. Their shoes matched their socks and belts (an axiom when I was first starting out), and although they were not what I would classify as dress shoes (they were mostly of the thicker-soled variety built more for wear and comfort than style), they were traditional looking and polished. If it wasn't for their Marine Corps haircuts, you would have thought they were an attachment of IBM salesmen from another era trapped in some kind of time warp. They looked neat and clean and competent, and they gained almost instant acceptance from everybody in the restaurant, who, generally speaking, couldn't take their eyes off the anachronistic happenstance.

As I sat there enjoying my bean curd bacon cheeseburger, I couldn't help but wonder why, as a profession, we ever gave up that arresting (pun intended) and proficient look. Oh sure, you still see the occasional pharmaceutical rep or a few other throwbacks still pounding the pavement in suits and ties, but even that modern interpretation of the traditional look, in many cases, has decomposed to a much more relaxed fit (read sloppy looking).

The deconstruction of formal business attire started with Casual Friday, where you could wear a nice pair of khaki pants and a sports shirt with a collar. Women's casual dress was less defined (isn't it always?), but along the same lines. Do you remember way back to the 20th century and that quaint concept? Now every day is casual day and the accepted dress by most managers is down several notches from those bygone frivolous Fridays, when we were presumably already in weekend mode.

Which was my problem with the whole concept in the first place. The message I got was, "We don't think you're going to work that hard on Friday anyway, so go ahead and dress the part." The way I learned it, your dress is a reflection of who you are, and since we're all selling ourselves (aren't we?), your choice of attire is usually the first impression you make when you meet a prospect (for those of us who still bother to make actual premise sales calls and don't spend all our time hiding behind an electronic persona). Judging by the less-than-sartorial splendor I see today among the sacred brotherhood of drummers, canvassers and knockers, it's no mystery figuring out the less-than-stellar state of sales out there on the street.

The quintessential idea is to represent yourself the best you can. If you want to establish credibility, reliability and honesty in the mind of your customer, at least start with a compelling package. When you're getting dressed in the morning, stop and ask yourself what your choice of clothes is going to say about you to your customers, your prospects and even your boss, who may not exactly be a Beau Brummel himself (I would write "herself" here, to be politically correct and all, but most women dress better than their male counterparts in the workplace, out of necessity; sad but true), but the foibles of sales management is a whole other subject for another time.

From a Not-So-Pasty Hippie of Yore

There's a story that's been going around for decades about a guy who owned a hot dog stand. You can find a few versions on the Internet if you dig deep enough, but they all have the same theme and lesson. My version is a composite of the many accounts I've heard and read over the years. I think the story is even more pertinent today in these batten-down-the-hatches and ride-out-the-economic-storm times we find ourselves still in the midst of, especially if you sell advertising like I do.

It seems there was a man who owned a hot dog stand called Harry's Hot Dog Heaven on a busy highway leading into Chicago, the hot dog capital of the world. Chicago hot dogs are famous and the best in the world. So what makes a Chicago hot dog so special? Here's how a website called *Hot Dog Chicago Style* describes it:

A Chicago Style Hot Dog is more than just a Hot Dog; it's a taste sensation with the perfect blend of toppings. A Chicago Style Hot Dog is never boiled, but slowly simmered using steam heat until the hot dog reaches approximately 170-180 degrees. A Chicago Style Hot Dog is topped with yellow mustard, bright green relish, onions, tomato wedges, pickle spear or slice, sport peppers and a dash of celery salt served in the all-important steamed poppy seed bun. The toppings are just as important as the order they are applied to the Hot Dog. If your Chicago Dog has been made properly, you will get a taste of each ingredient in every bite.

And they're great. If you've ever had a Chicago hot dog—in Chicago!—you know what I'm talking about. If you haven't, quite frankly, you've never had a real hot dog, as far as I'm concerned. I've had Chicago hot dogs in other places around the country, but they're never as good as the ones in Chicago, just like Philadelphia cheese steaks are never as good as the ones you get in Philly. (And don't fall for that Pat's versus Gino's, tourist-trap malarkey; go to Jim's Steaks on South Street where all the hippies meet, according to The Orlons hit record from 1963—look it up! Or, if you really want the best cheese steak in the civilized world, and I use the word "civilized" here with some reservations, go to the White House in Atlantic City. I know it's not in Philly, but close enough. Get yourself a cheese steak or hoagie, a soda, bag of chips, and top it off with a Tastykake lemon pie. Mmm, mmm good! There's no finer dining on this entire green/blue ball.)

But I digress.

Harry's business was booming. People couldn't get enough of his delicious hot dogs, made with the finest ingredients and prepared perfectly with great love and care. Harry kept the business open long hours each day in order to catch all the commuter and transient traffic. He advertised on directional billboards, placed coupon offers in the newspaper twice a week, and ran a spot with a clever jingle on a few of Chicago's top radio stations. Harry's employees were trained and managed properly, well paid and loved their jobs. As a result of Harry's industriousness and thoroughness, he was raking it in, raking it in to the point where he could afford to send his son to one of the finest universities back east where young Harry Jr. earned an Ivy League MBA.

His father was so proud! Harry had barely made it out of high school, but here was his son with a master's degree in business. Graduation day was one of the happiest days of Harry's life.

When young Harry returned to Chicago, he sat his father down and told him a recession was on its way and he had to make some adjustments in order to weather the storm. He told his father that all the indicators and experts pointed toward a protracted and difficult period of a soft economy, and that it would have a devastating effect on many small businesses.

Harry was greatly impressed by his learned son with an Ivy League MBA. "What should I do?" he asked young Harry.

"The first thing you need to do is cut your advertising in half. It's expensive, and the savings will help you with your cash flow."

"Cash flow," Harry thought. My son is truly an economic genius.

So Harry cut back on his advertising, and after a couple of months, business, as his wise son had predicted, began to slip. Harry went back to his son to ask for advice, and his son told him to cancel all his advertising immediately and cut back on his hours of operations. Harry obediently followed his son's advice, and, as foretold, business got even worse. So impressed with his son's insight, Harry asked him what he should do next.

"Lay off employees and cut back on the quality of the ingredients you're buying" was guidance Harry could not ignore from such a bright and knowledgeable source. So once more, Harry complied with his son's directions, and, before long, Harry's Hot Dog Heaven went out of business. Harry couldn't believe how astute and perceptive his devoted son was to forecast the demise of the business.

So the next time some BMW'd, Rolex'd, Brooks Brothers all-of-that is telling you about his Wharton or Harvard School of Business MBA, tell him it's hard to beat a tube of meat, but you think he's got it well in hand.

Words Are All I Have, Part 1

A couple of weeks ago I was traveling, and while stopped at a red light in an unfamiliar town, noticed a business on the opposite side of the street named Eccola Restaurant. At first blush I thought I had read E. coli Restaurant. I was dumbstruck. I quickly realized it actually read Eccola, but I was still in disbelief. I sat in my car staring, trying to get my brain around the concept of this unusual and suggestive name until the thoughtful and helpful New Jersey drivers reminded me the light had changed to green.

As soon as I got back to the hotel, I Googled Eccola and found that it's an Italian adverb meaning "here it is."

Here it is, indeed, just maybe the worst name I've ever heard for a restaurant.Thanks to the overly hysterical, panic-inducing, 24/7 media coverage of the most insignificant minutia of our daily existence here on the third planet from the sun, we all know that E. coli is a dangerous, life-threatening blight perpetrated by money-grubbing profiteers. In reality, most forms of E. coli are harmless and actually provide a benefit. But truth and the mundane workings of the world will never get in the way of a really good national frenzy in this age of multiple messages, bombarding us constantly as they flash, crawl, pop-up and slam into our over-worked, over-stimulated, over-exploited psyches, pulsing from the ubiquitous viewing screens of our 52-inch HD, 3-D TVs or our tiny smart phone that we can't read outside in the sun. (The pain and suffering of modern times!) You can't even pump gas without a viewing screen hovering over you like Big Brother, always there, always watching. (Aren't they? Or is the medication losing effect?)

Eccola is probably one of those neat little Italian bistros where you bring your own Chianti and they yell your order into the kitchen while *Pagliacci* plays in the background, where the veal is tender and flavorful and the homemade marinara sauce is to die for. But I ain't no fool; I'm not eating nowhere they serve E. coli.

As I was told on my first job interview by a critical and petulant personnel manager, choose your words carefully, which is very good advice. Words are powerful tools that can help or harm you, depending on your skills and intentions. Words are the true weapons of mass destruction, but words can also lift hearts and make spirits soar. In the end, words are all we really have, especially if you're in sales. For a salesperson, what you say is who you are. What you say is how your product or service is perceived. What you say is the difference between success or failure, the difference between making money and not making money, the difference between feeling good about yourself or feeling like a limp wad of lint floating in the wind, blown from one lost opportunity to another—always the victim, never the victor.

Choosing words carefully and using effective power-words that call for immediate action was a lesson drummed into me over the years. I learned that we never ask a client to sign a contract because people don't like or trust contracts, and they never want to sign anything. Isn't that what your attorney from the law firm Whiplash R Us preaches to you? "Don't sign nottin, babe, cause you can't trust nobody. Trust me," as he flashes his gold-front-tooth smile, stomps his cloven foot and flips his spiked tail for emphasis. Instead, we ask our clients to okay the agreement or initiate the order. And when we give a price, no matter if it's ridiculously, astronomically high, we always preface it with the word "only."

Always! As in, "That half-inch widget made of recycled glue, balsa wood and hope is only $19,999.99. Will that be cash or check?"

Words are all we have, so use them wisely. We're all taught this from the first day we get into sales, but unfortunately, many latter-day Willy Lomans are too busy talking and don't hear what's being said, so the words they choose are often unrelated to the needs or concerns of the prospect. Countless sales are stillborn every day because of careless, superfluous words. It is written that Samson slew thousands of Philistines with the jawbone of an ass, and it is said that thousands of sales are killed every day with the same weapon. As Joe Jones sang in his 1960 hit, "You talk too much you worry me to death, you talk too much you even worry my pet, you just talk, talk, talk too much."

So don't talk too much, and when you do talk, talk smart. The use and arrangement of words can be the key to the kingdom.

Or not.

Like good old moo cow milk.

Words Are All I Have, Part 2

Is the bird really the word?

It may very well be for Peter Griffin of *Family Guy* fame, but for the rest of us, especially those carrying a bag and pounding the pavement, the word is definitely much, much more than the bird (although its representative gesture is what we often feel like flipping our clients and prospects). As I previously wrote, words are all we really have; they're our sword and shield against the fire-breathing dragons of resistance, rejection and repudiation of our mortal souls; they are our tools, our mortar, our bricks, and how we use them will determine whether we return from the field of battle with our banner flying high or our tail tucked between our legs (in a frenzied mix of splintered and cluttered metaphors).

I learned at an early age the problems words can cause if you don't keep your guard up every minute; one slight misstep and all of a sudden you're an idiot, or worse, some kind of pervert. I must have been 11 or 12 years old and was having dinner at a friend's house.

During the meal, his parents and sister (who was much older than us, probably 16 or 17) were talking about a piece of carpet they had looked at earlier in the day in a shop that specialized in Persian rugs. Coincidentally, we had just learned in school how rugs are made, and we had watched a slide show on people weaving a Persian rug. I couldn't wait to jump into the conversation and tell them all I knew about Persian rugs. Oh boy, was I going to look smart.

Or, as it turned out, not so smart.

"We learned all about Persian rugs in school," I announced, completely thrilled with myself. Pete, my friend, cocked his head to one side and scrunched up his mouth in a look that said, "What the heck are you doing?"

"We saw pictures that showed people making them," I continued, undeterred. "They were weaving them on a womb."

The table went silent. Pete looked at me in disbelief. I didn't know what was up, and then his parents and sister started laughing.

"I think you mean they weave them on a loom," his mother said, throwing me a life preserver I didn't know I needed.

"It's a common mistake," his father added, and the room erupted in loud laughter once again. Later that night, when Pete told me what I had said and what it meant, I had a post-traumatic-humiliation-meltdown. I was horrified, mortified, traumatized. As Billy Joel would sing years later, "You had to open up your mouth, you had to be a big shot, didn't you." As a matter of fact, I did, and I never went back to Pete's house again.

You think I would have learned my lesson, but not this boy. Fast forward 40 years to a boardroom in the middle of a smoldering July afternoon in Winston-Salem, North Carolina. I am sitting at a large, oval table surrounded by five men directly out of William Faulkner's Snopes family trilogy, buggy eyed and curious in appearance and demeanor. At the head of the table presides Big Daddy himself, dressed in a dark three-piece suit on this pleasant day in Hades, sporting a show-stopping, full head of thick, snow-white hair. The man is a mountain, solid and rooted to his spot of prominence, as he stares at me in a benign but troubling manner. He has yet to say a word other than a short, perfunctory greeting.

The purpose of the meeting is irrelevant to the subject of this story other than I was trying to sell them something of great value. The other four men are younger and more or less engaged in the meeting, as engaged as they could be between darting nervous looks at Big Daddy to check his reaction every time something is said, which is imperceptible to me. They are friendly in an oddly friendly way, if you know what I mean. They aren't really polite but more proper and awkwardly respectful; not really welcoming but solicitous in a peculiarly guarded manner.

It was a weird scene and I was definitely not grooving on the colliding vibes, so I did what I always do in that type of situation to try and lighten the tension: I started talking about the most interesting and stimulating thing I knew.

Me.

I owned and operated a business in North Carolina for several years and would fly in and out of Greensboro on a fairly regular basis. However, once a year we would pack up the family and make a road trip out of it. On this particular trip, we were on a Civil War tour, and that's what I started talking about on that stifling, *Deliverance*-like afternoon, sitting in a boardroom that oozed an ominous warning, like the soulful sound of the lighthouse bell ringing on a dark, foggy night. I was creeped out, so I talked faster, trying to sweep them along in my enthusiasm and excitement.

I told them all about my fascination and love of Civil War history. I described our tour of Manassas, the site of the first real battle of the war, better known as Bull Run, and how the gentry of Washington had sat on hills surrounding the battlefield, eating picnic lunches as men were brutally blown to pieces in front of them. I talked about all the great Civil War places to visit in Virginia, and how much we were enjoying the trip. I talked about Appomattox and described how I felt standing in the room where General Robert E. Lee had surrendered to General Ulysses S. Grant, and I told them we were going to cap off the trip with a few days in Gettysburg, the most fascinating battle in history, in my humble opinion.

After I had gone on for some time, I stopped to catch my breath and noticed the looks of panic on the four cornpones' faces.

Big Daddy was smiling at me in a look of bemused amusement. He ceremoniously cleared his throat as if he was going to say something of momentous importance. The knuckleheads-four looked like they were going to collectively pee themselves.

"Do you refer, sir, to the war of northern aggression?" he finally said. It was not a question, it was an accusation.

I was dead in the water, and no revolving, piercing beacon or warning bell could save me from crashing on the rocks of my own undisciplined, overindulgent hubris.

Choose your words carefully, indeed. And know your audience. Another fine lesson learned just a wee bit too late. The words we use can cause so much damage, even the ones delivered with the best of intentions, like the two, four-letter ones that threw my seventh-grade classmates of the male persuasion into a debilitating tizzy and crippled milk consumption for an entire town.

Words Are All I Have, Part 3

Did you ever notice that you can say a lot of incredibly poignant, moving things (in your mind, anyway) that never seem to get heard, but make one little slip, and you're toast? You can silver-tongue a string of perfect pearls on your prospect, palaver over the finer, relevant features and benefits of your product, dance her around the Maypole of glittering, cascading images while spinning multi-stimulating pictures of across-the-board, utilitarian value, but throw one inadvertent, minor boner in there and it's "Wham, bam, thank you ma'am!" You're history. You're lost at sea and the Coast Guard rescue helicopter just went home for lunch as you dip for your final farewell beneath the insurmountable waves of the perfect storm of your own making. They're throwing the last few shovels-ful of dirt over your stiff, lifeless corpse as the band plays "This is the last worthless evening that you'll have to spend."

Goodbye yellow brick road; hello junk pile of lost opportunity.

Words, man. Words can kill you, so really, just shut up. It's the best advice I can give, but it's incredibly hard to do. I find myself, in times of awkwardness or during a nervous pause, starting to talk too much, and talk too fast, and talk, talk, talk right into the pigeon-hole of "just another fast-talking, disingenuous sales hack."

Oh, brother, it's a hard, hard road *we few, we happy few* toil along to earn our daily bread, especially when they start moving the stakes and changing the meaning of words to make our modest efforts even more arduous. The interesting thing about sales is that no matter how tough it gets, there's always some Maalox-chugging, tight-ass interloper just waiting for the opportunity to make it even tougher. And as difficult as it is to find good salespeople, it's startlingly easy to find buttoned-down frauds.

I was exposed in college to those kind of miscommunications and the frightened, weak-kneed-willies who hide behind deliberate misdirections, creating a smoke-screen of twisted, mangled nomenclature to mask their own deficiencies. I went to Rutgers Camden in New Jersey, where William Lutz was a professor. Lutz is one of the leading authorities on doublespeak, a bastardized Orwellian concept that Wikipedia describes as "language that deliberately disguises, distorts, or reverses the meaning of words. Doublespeak may take the form of euphemisms (e.g., 'downsizing' for layoffs), making the truth less unpleasant, without denying its nature. It may also be deployed as intentional ambiguity, or reversal of meaning (for example, naming a state of war 'peace'). In such cases, doublespeak disguises the nature of the truth, producing a communication bypass."

Communication bypass, huh? I hope Wikipedia is being ironic there, because I don't know what the hell a communication bypass is.

You can Google "Lutz" or "doublespeak" and get lots of material and examples, some funny, some stupid, some transparent and some that will scare the living daylights out of you. My favorites, however, are the ones used in business. (Go figure.)

I worked for a Fortune 100 company in New York City a few lifetimes ago, and they loved using any new euphemisms or buzz word that appeared on the horizon. They lapped up every novel concept that came down the pike, and used them effectively, I thought, to keep anyone from noticing that they had no clue how to drive the company. I remember when "empowerment" was all the rage, and they couldn't resist making it their very own. The idea was to make employees think they had some control over their situation by ostensibly allowing them to participate in the formulation of their responsibilities and the direction of the team or department. In reality, their ideas were accepted if they agreed with the company's philosophy and management's agenda. Otherwise, they were ignored. The real truth was that instead of empowering anybody, the program encouraged employees to lower their guard and be even more vulnerable to management, who promptly used the opportunity to further manipulate and abuse them. It was a swell idea that still has some legs today. As a word of caution, though, if your boss ever tells you he wants to empower you, just say no.

My favorite misdirection of simple language was employed by the same company. The office I worked in was on the 35th floor of a building on Madison Avenue, and it was primarily staffed by executive management and high-level sales folk. Whenever one of those indispensable links (as we were often told we were) was fired, a memo would go forth (before email and text messaging) that so-and-so had been promoted to Special Projects and would be working on the tenth floor, or some other barren wasteland where the broken and superfluous were relegated. Can you believe the audacity? The special project was to find another job, but they actually positioned it as a promotion, even though everybody knew exactly what they were talking about.

Whatayatalk, whatayataalk, whatayatalk?

Pearl Harbor is another of my favorites for bending words to achieve a new and different meaning for an old idea that has worn out its welcome. When I was growing up, not too long after World War II, we were taught that Pearl Harbor was sneak attacked. Years later, as the Japanese government became our ally and the new Detroit, we were told Pearl Harbor was subject to a surprise attack. At first blush, you may see little difference between "sneak" and "surprise," but the chasm between the two connotations is as wide as the Grand Canyon. A sneak attack sounds despicable and loathsome while a surprise attack sounds militarily sound. If you don't think there's much of a difference between the two, what images do these two sentences create in your mind?

"A man came home early and surprised his wife."

"A man surprised his wife by sneaking home early."

One sounds like a fun, unexpected afternoon, and the other sounds like a fun but abbreviated afternoon with possible residual ramifications of a tragic nature (what with the gunfire and all).

Words. They can mean whatever you want them to mean, so make them mean what you want them to mean. Not like the ones that could ruin a young boy's cream donut on his way to school in the morning.

Words Are All I Have, Conclusion

Word, dog?

Well, it happened like this:

It was the fall of 1960 and Elvis was king, *The Magnificent Seven* was a box office smash, *Bonanza* was being beamed into the rich folk's living rooms in full (if not somewhat muted and distorted) color, Roy Orbison's "Only the Lonely" was a big-boss hit, Kennedy would be elected president, and during those lazy, hazy, crazy days of summer, I had discovered girls and football. I learned that one smelled unbelievably good in a heavenly, magical, love-potion vapor that made my knees go weak, and the other smelled unbelievably bad in a mix of sweat, Bengay and foot fungus powder that made my knees unusable decades later. It's still a photo-finish as to which smell I loved more, and a whiff of either transports me back to those days of discovery, mystery and ecstasy. And silly, childish ignorance.

I grew up in Riverton, New Jersey, a small town of 5,000 predominantly white Christians, on the banks of the Delaware River, across the dirty waters from North Philadelphia and all those teased-hair, gum-popping, tight-sweatered GUDs (geographically undesirable girls, we were taught with inflexible conviction). Riverton, New Jersey, was straight out of a Norman Rockwell painting, with the same feel, texture and two-dimensional depth. There were numerous churches in and around town for your weekly fix of judgmental self-righteousness and sanctimonious disapproval, and lots of white picket fences, built low and easy to navigate over in the dark of night when coveting thy neighbor's wife would simply no longer feed the bulldog. It was an idyllic setting for a 13 year-old-boy destined to grow up with a semi-cynical perspective, a purveyor of humorous irony with a sardonic twist. These were fertile, fallow fields to help shape and sharpen a skewed vision of the world as we were taught it should be by *Father Knows Best* and *Leave It to Beaver*, our real preachers and shamans in those post-war, pre-Watergate years of continental self-denial.

And Riverton, New Jersey, was all of that in 1960. It was a dry town, meaning you couldn't purchase alcohol of any variety within the town's geographic limits. No bars, liquor stores or beer distributors, just churches and white picket fences, beaming out our collective self-satisfaction at being better than everybody else. But there were three places in town where you could knock back a couple of cold ones over a poker game, or discuss the fluctuating market prices while sampling a single malt scotch whiskey, or sip a snifter or two with your old fraternity buddy: the firehouse, the country club or the yacht club, and where you drank was determined by your placement within the town's rigid and well-defined social strata. My family hung at the firehouse, just so you know who you're dealing with.

Riverton, New Jersey, was like one of those little towns you build around a miniature train set under a Christmas tree. We had an A&P grocery store on the edge of town, our one concession to modern living. Malls had yet to take over Main Street, USA, (and yes, we had a Main Street, which intersected with Broad Street in the middle of town), and in 1960, Riverton, New Jersey, had not changed a great deal in 100 years. We had Keating's Drug Store with a real soda fountain counter and the best ham sandwiches I've ever had, where you could lay down the occasional bet (before the state took over the numbers racket and sanitized its image by calling it the Lottery). There was a small grocery store on Main Street that later became a five-and-dime with a Coca Cola vending machine out front on the sidewalk that we could reach into with our skinny, nimble arms and twist them up into the guts of the brightly lit, boxy apparatus to liberate a sweet, syrupy, cold treat on a hot summer night. We had a barber shop (where my grandfather worked), a butcher with sawdust on the floor and his thumb on the scale, a bike shop, a produce store, a thrift shop, a shoemaker, and two wonderful, home-to-a-young-boy's-greatest-adventures lumber yards (because this was the post-war boom era when you couldn't build things fast enough). There was a bank constructed of sturdy, reliable stone, a dry cleaner with a huge neon sign, and a couple of gas stations that held a certain intrigue to those of us who valued almost anything greasy, especially if it was made of shiny steel.

Down Main Street, a couple blocks from Broad, sat Sharon's Sweet Shop, where I wasted every minute I could hanging out with my pals and eating French fries with too much salt and way too much ketchup. That's where we learned all about the workings of the world from things we talked about and shared, which was 80 percent hogwash intended to impress or intimidate each other. It was the center of my universe and there wasn't a happier place on earth in those times of youthful exhilaration, except Klippel's Bakery.

Ah, Klippel's Bakery. The memory still brings a smile to my face. They made the best snowflake rolls. I can't describe them with any justice, but if you want a treat, get yourself a time machine and go back to Klippel's, buy a snowflake roll (for maybe a nickel), put on some Miracle Whip with baloney and a slice of American cheese and you'll know what I'm talking about. The feast of a 13 year-old-Don Juan/Jim Brown in waiting.

The snowflake rolls were your mama's pajamas, for sure, but it was their cream donuts that drove me around the bend (or more accurately, across the tracks). Klippel's was situated on the southwest corner of Broad and Main, and you couldn't get to Riverton Public School from the east side of town without crossing the railroad tracks (that ran along Broad) and passing Klippel's. Every single day on your way to school. What was a boy to do? Stop and buy a cream donut, of course, and maybe a pint of chocolate milk from the milk machine in Klippel's parking lot next to the side door that led into the kitchen.

In Riverton, New Jersey, in 1960, as in most towns across America in 1960, the fire whistle blew at 5:00 PM and all commerce of the day came to a halt. The stores were locked up, including the A&P, and home you went for supper—never dinner with candles and a fine imported wine; this was a sit-down, say your prayers, meat and potatoes, cook 'em 'til you kill all traces of nutrients supper. And if, by chance, you needed something from the store after 5:00 PM, you were SOL (like WTF, but back before we used acronyms and phonetic sounds to communicate electronically, now leaking over into our vernacular—sort of like going back to our roots when cavemen grunted and used simple sounds to express themselves—the final deconstruction of language and the repudiation of all words more than two undemanding syllables, the apocalyptic trade-off of harmonious effectiveness for artificial efficiency).

Unless you needed milk. If you needed milk, you sent your son on his bike to Klippel's to buy a quart of milk from the milk machine in Klippel's parking lot next to the side door to the kitchen. If a son wasn't available for reasons of proximity or sperm propulsion failure, you could send your daughter, but only if absolutely necessary and there were absolutely no other viable contingency scenarios for the procurement of the liquid by-product of sward-ingesting, female-gendered mammals of the bovine variety (just a little doublespeak to keep you on your toes). If only that last-ditch-effort contingency plan had been in effect in the fall of 1960, the borough of Riverton, New Jersey, wouldn't have had to suffer the Great Post-5:00 PM Milk Deficiency that inexplicably gripped the town for the better part of a week.

During that fateful week, life went on as usual, and as usual, boys would be dispatched occasionally after 5:00 PM on their trusty bikes to fetch a quart of milk from Klippel's. But the boys were returning home empty handed with lowered, sheepish eyes and flimsy excuses, like the machine was out of milk, which didn't make a lot of sense because there were three portals on the milk machine, two for quarts of milk and one for pints of chocolate milk. As the days went by and young boys continued to come home milkless, it became the talk of the town. Mothers would stop at Klippel's during their daytime errands to complain about the problem, but the good folks at Klippel's would tell them that the machine was fully stocked and operating properly and they didn't have a clue what was going on.

Finally, one evening after a nervous boy returned home *sans* milk, his dad put him in the car and drove to Klippel's. As soon as they got to the machine, his dad started laughing out loud. Being a veteran of World War II and a man of the world, he understood immediately the problem at hand. His son looked at him in bewilderment but the dad couldn't stop laughing.

Above the three portals on the machine were plastic holders where you slipped in cardboard placards to designate what product was available from each portal. The signs were printed by the milk supplier and inserted by the drivers when they made their deliveries. Apparently the placards had become badly faded to the point where you could barely read them, and the driver, during one of his stops to refill the machine, decided to hand print new signs so at least people could see what they were buying. However, there wasn't much room on the placards, and "homogenized" is a big word, so the driver simply abbreviated it to read "Homo Milk."

End of mystery. No young boy in Riverton, New Jersey, in the fall of 1960 was going to drink homo milk, regardless of his sexual orientation or preferences. It just wasn't something you would do back then, and although we now live in a more enlightened age where most clear-thinking people understand that sexual orientation is not a lifestyle choice, in 1960 we weren't thinking along those lines and we weren't taking any chances. No way, no how.

Not that there's anything wrong with that.

This is a true story. I may have enhanced it a bit, which, according to Bobby Brown, is my prerogative, but it really happened. If I offended anybody, I apologize. That wasn't my intention. My intention was to show how easily words can be misunderstood and ideas can get lost in the cascading downpour of harmful, inaccurate oratory. So please be careful what you say, and what you write, if you want people to understand you and buy your product.

Enlightenment or not, however, I'm still not eating E. coli or drinking homo milk. I'm guessing any E. coli bacteria that makes its way into my body is going to be a product of the harmful side of the genetic crap-shoot, and homogenized, whole milk contains way too much fat for me. I prefer 2 percent low fat, or even soy milk, with my cereal in the morning.

Speaking of which, I miss those cream donuts for breakfast. As a matter of fact, one sure would taste great right about now with a tall class of ice-cold homo milk.

A Rose by Any Other Name

Speaking of doublespeak, did you ever notice all the names used to identify salespeople? It's almost funny how far people and companies will go to not use the word salesman, or salesperson. That's because nobody wants to be a salesperson. I certainly didn't. As I write in Chapter 1 of *How to Sell the Plague*, "Yeah, like I wanted to be a salesman. Right. Big smile, firm handshake and shiny shoes, *à la* Willie Loman; slap you on the back and tell-you-what-I'm-gonna-do, fast-talking, no-low-is-too-low creeps. Not me, pal. No way."

Even after I decided I wanted a sales job, I still couldn't view it as anything less than consorting with the Devil, as I describe my feelings at that point. "Like an old-time Fourth of July, fireworks explode in my head, bands play gay, snappy Sousa marches and young girls in body-tight, sparkling singlets pass by, throwing batons high over their heads, and here I sit in the open Cadillac convertible, smiling and waving to the happy, smiling denizen of the brave new world that was just opened up to me; brand new, freshly minted, here for your inspection, capitalist extraordinaire, clean-shaven, *bang beat, bell ringing, big haul, great go, neck or nothing, rip roaring, every time a bull's eye* salesman-to-be, Professor Harold Hill incarnate, future purveyor of all things money can buy, reborn spirit of American consumerism, betrayer of principles, fallen keeper of the flame."

I have heard from numerous salespeople who tell me they felt the same way when they got into sales and can identify with the terror and anxiety I felt when I took that first, fateful step. Those cold sweats are the result of a long history of snake oil salesmen who still slither among us today. We of the small but confident group of the initiated souls of the forever shifting brotherhood of drummers, canvassers and knockers are forever burdened with the images of Professor Marvel from *The Wizard of Oz* to scumbag extraordinaire Bernie Madoff, and one of the ways we try to compensate for that debilitating characterization is to call ourselves anything but salesmen or saleswomen. I once worked with a guy who was a sales trainer, and he made a lot of money being a sales trainer, and he lived a very nice lifestyle because he made a lot of money being a sale trainer, but I never heard him once refer to himself as a sales trainer. On his business card, he called himself a Marketing Resource Counselor. Like I said, it's almost funny, and might be if it wasn't so pathetic.

And sad.

Do you remember the original *Wall Street* movie? In a fun example of life imitating art, Martin Sheen plays Charlie Sheen's father and has this exchange with him:

<u>Carl (Martin Sheen)</u> *I told you not to go into that racket.*
You could've been a doctor or a lawyer.
<u>Bud (Charlie Sheen)</u> *Coulda been a contender.*
<u>Carl (continuing)</u> *You coulda stayed at Bluestar and been a supervisor instead of going off and bein' a salesman.*
<u>Bud</u> *Look Dad, I'm not a salesman. How many times I gotta tell you I'm an account executive, and pretty soon I'm going to the investment banking side of the firm.*
<u>Carl</u> *You get on the phone and ask strangers for their money, right? You're a salesman.*

Oh, what an insult! Can you imagine a father calling his son a salesman? Talk about child abuse. (Which may explain a few peculiar things in Charlie's life. I mean, how do you recover from being called a salesman by your father?)

That's why we never use the S word. My favorites are insurance and car salespeople. Insurance guys will go to any length to convince you they're not trying to sell you insurance. They call themselves Financial Advisors, or Financial Planners, or Investment Analysts, or Portfolio Consultants—anything, as long as the title doesn't contain the words insurance or sales. And car guys, they're the best. They can be anything from a Vehicle Procurement Advisor to a Customer Care Specialist. Customer care? You've got to be kidding. First and foremost, at most dealerships their care goes as far as selling you a car, and when the time comes in a few weeks where the trunk pops open every time you turn on the radio, the only thing they'll be caring about is when's lunch.

How about a little honesty in place of misdirection and deceiving doublespeak? At some point during a sales call (and yes, they are sales calls), I will often tell clients to please remember I'm in sales and it's my job to try to sell them my products. That's how I get paid. I do this to help separate myself from the rest of the herd pretending to be advisors. It breaks the tension and puts the prospect at ease. At worst, at least they know I'm honest, and that allows them to let go of some of the automatic barriers that shoot up during a solicitation (and yes, it's a solicitation). I then proceed to convince them through my behavior and recommendations that I really am looking out for their best interests (which I am). In the end, I sell more that way and really do end up helping my clients.

We are not consultants, we are not advisors, we are not counselors. We are salespeople. We make our money selling. As I've written before, if you can sell more being any of those things, then by all means, wear those cloaks and veils, but don't forget how you make money. All I do is tell my clients the truth, and that is I'm a salesman.

Sales trainers call that a pattern interrupt (they love to make up really cool names for things you do every day and then charge you through the nose for the mundane and the obvious), but that makes it sound like a technique or gimmick. However, honesty is neither; it's the only real basis for an ongoing, productive relationship for both parties.

So, let's start with a little truthfulness in what we call ourselves, instead of all the manipulative and mutated monikers we go by. In my career, I've been known as a Directory Advertising Sales Representative, Advertising Representative, Account Executive, Advertising Sales Consultant, Field Sales Representative, Business Development Manager, and Media Consultant. Actually, I've been called everything but a salesman, but that's exactly what I am. The problem is, when we go to so much trouble to create all those euphemisms, it makes it sound like we're ashamed of what we do to earn our daily bread. But I'm not apologizing for who I am. Like The Who's "Baba O'Riley," "Out here in the fields, I fight for my meals, I get my back into my living. I don't need to fight to prove I'm right, I don't need to be forgiven."

Lap Dances Are Not Expensible

"Money, honey, that's what I want," is what I write in Chapter 1 of *How to Sell the Plague* when describing my primary motivation for getting into sales. Okay, a lot of water has cascaded over that bullet-hole-riddled dam since those halcyon days of naive enchantment, and I know now that money had almost nothing to do with it, as it almost always has nothing to do with anything after you boil things down to the heat-seared stain in the middle of a saucepan left on a hot burner too long after all the water has evaporated into an unpleasant, humid vapor. But still, give me the money, please—I'll deal with the allegorical implications later.

And I'll take that moolah and its hedonistic remunerations in any form I can get, like a nice, fat expense account. I started thinking about expense accounts and my interesting experiences with them over the years after seeing a really cool video on YouTube. It's titled "A Few Good Expenses," and please watch it.

Now.

I'll wait.

I told you it was cool. Of course, it's only cool if you've seen *A Few Good Men*, one of my favorite movies. I think it includes the best performances ever turned in by Tom Cruise, Jack Nicholson, Demi Moore, Kevin Bacon, Kevin Pollak and Kiefer Sutherland. If you haven't seen the movie, watch it.

Not now.

I can't wait that long.

However, the "A Few Good Expenses" video will be much funnier if you know what's going on, which is true of most jokes, but not all. Like Washington, the locale of the movie and the video. You don't really need to know anything about the hijinks perpetrated on that converted swampland to get the ongoing and never-ending joke. That's because we're invariably the butt of the joke, of course.

But I digress.

Expense accounts have always been a raw nerve between accounting and sales. To a lot of bean counters, sales itself is an unnecessary expense, and most of the company outside of sales often see us *happy few* as *grotesque and incomprehensible*. I like it like that; I like being mysterious and unknowable, feared and loathed, out on the street, closing sales and generating revenue that they *rise and sleep under*. I like being the go-to guy who keeps the wheels turning. And sometimes those wheels need greasing.

My favorite wheel greasing occurred in Toronto about 25 years ago. I was working for a large out-of-home advertising company out of New York City, but the division I represented had their headquarters in Toronto, where my boss was officed. We printed posters for billboards and produced large-formatted, vinyl displays for highway signs. I had taken a client up to the plant in Canada to tour the facilities and view the process, and my boss and I took him out to dinner that night. We went to a posh restaurant in downtown Toronto and had a great meal. Afterwards, we sidled up to the bar and ordered Louis XIV. Three snifters of cognac at a clip of $60 per. That was 180 buckaroos in 1980s dollars. Guess whose expense account that little excess ended up on? If you guessed "Not your boss's," you win! The story became a company legend, but one usually told with pure venom and green-eyed jealousy. The client ended up spending about a quarter of a million dollars a year with us, money that paid the salaries of many of the support people who glared at me with the aforementioned fear and loathing on my subsequent visits. It was fascinating, in a perverse sort of way, that I could make that many people hate me while helping them keep gainful employment. What a conundrum!

And ironic. I traveled a great deal with that job, and coming from a world of small-ball sales where every penny was scrutinized, I would generally stay at less expensive hotels. Marriott had recently introduced Courtyards and they were clean, modern and cheap, so I stayed there as often as I could. After a couple of months of that kind of frugality, I was sure the company was noticing.

They were.

I was called into the CEO's office and told I was not staying at nice enough (read expensive enough) hotels. He didn't want me giving our customers the impression we were impoverished or cheap, so I was given a list of approved hotels around the country, all four star, top-of-the-line facilities. He didn't exactly tell me to order Louis XIV, but he made it clear I was supposed to conduct myself in a manner that spoke of prosperity and class, and what could show more class than drinking Louis XIV. So I was simply doing my job as instructed.

A few years earlier, I was working in Philadelphia in national sales. We had a rep who also covered national sales from a New York office, and when I started with that company, he took me aside at lunch one day and told me that whenever I turned in an expense, I had to add 25 percent to cover my extra operating costs that never show up on an expense report. I wasn't sure what those extra costs were exactly, so I disregarded that bit of advice. A year or so later, after the other rep had left the company, my boss told me his expenses were twice as high as mine, and that he had tried to get me to pad my expense report so he wouldn't look so bad. Very shrewd, and very interesting because years later the other rep had his own company where I did some consulting, and every time I turned in a bill with my itemized expenses, he would go over it with a fine-toothed comb, looking for that extra 25 percent, I guess.

At that same job, I got into a discussion one day with another salesman over putting in a $1 expense item for some magazines I had purchased. Did I read them for my own enjoyment? Yes, I did. Did I also use them as a source of advertising leads? Yes to that one too, so I saw it as a legitimate expense. I wouldn't have bought them purely for my own entertainment, and I needed them for my job. I said something about it only being a dollar, and this pious little Boy Scout responded with, "Well, how much does it have to be before it's stealing?"

Leapfrog ahead a few months when my partner and I were scrambling for an extra $50,000 in billing by year's end to make our annual bonus. Our job was to handle all national business that either walked in the door or that we generated; local reps were not allowed to handle anything that was considered a national account, like Tyson Chicken. I got word on the street that Tyson was making a big national buy that included Philadelphia and that it would be right around $50,000. What a gift from the gods, but, as it turned out, the sanctimonious turd-boy intercepted the call coming into the office and hijacked the sale. It ended up on his account list before anybody in the company knew about it. After the larceny was discovered, the sales manager refused to slap down the brown-nosing sycophant and let him keep the business. He justified it by saying that the mealy-mouthed dust ball had done all the work on the account. What work? He answered the freaking phone! We made our bonus in spite of that piracy (another great story for another time), and I had the wonderful opportunity to tell the little jasper that I was pretty sure $50,000 constituted stealing.

Years later, I was at an industry convention in Baltimore when I found myself at the bar one night, sipping a beer and enjoying the robust camaraderie of my fellow salespeople from around the region. There was a guy there I'll call Al who was the Senior Vice President of Sales for a medium-sized, out-of-home advertising company, and he had a reputation for being a bit of a drinker. The guy was a falling-down drunk. Someone that night, as Al degenerated into his usual fog, found out Al's room number, and for the rest of the evening, everybody's drinks were charged to Al's room. A couple of days later we were all gone when Al finally checked out. He must have been surprised; I heard the bill was several thousand dollars. How he got it through finance, I don't know, but Al was a slick salesman and I'm sure he pulled it off.

On another industry-famous evening, I'm guessing even Al's practiced slick wouldn't stick. The story is told that Al got stinking drunk one night and picked up a lady of the evening. Apparently he took her back to the office and proceeded to undress and lie on the boardroom table naked as a jaybird, where he passed out cold. When he woke up in the early hours of the morning, the girl was gone. So, too, were his clothes and his company car.

You may be able to finesse the occasional lap dance or Louis XIV past your boss, your bookkeeper and the IRS, but I'm pretty sure you cannot sneak through a hooker and a car. I mean, you have to draw the line somewhere.

Mitch & Murray Sent Me

"A-B-C. A-Always, B-Be, C-Closing. Always be closing, always be closing."

If you haven't seen *Glengary Glen Ross* and you consider yourself a salesperson, then you've missed an interesting and provocative portrayal of how the world at large views our happy, overworked and underappreciated band of brothers and sisters. The movie portrays us as lowlife scum who will do anything to make a sale, regardless of what ethics or morals we may have to bend in order to close the deal. "Always be closing," as mouthed by the character Blake (played by Alec Baldwin) is the supposed mantra of all us slimy and disingenuous drummers, knockers and peddlers.

Mitch and Murray are the off-screen owners of the company who have sent Blake, their presumed top gun, out into the field to bully and abuse the other salesmen into working harder and even more ruthlessly. The film is full of great quotes that I can't repeat in a family-oriented book, but please do yourself a favor and watch it.

Based on a play of the same name by David Mamet, you could spend a lifetime studying the psychological allegories represented by Mitch, Murray and Blake. Actually, a sales trainer told me he once taught an entire 12-week class dissecting the movie.

I've been thinking about that movie and Blake since reading *Delivering Happiness* by Tony Hsieh. Hsieh (pronounced Shay) is the CEO of Zappos, and if you're not a fashionista or metrosexual, you probably have no idea what Zappos is. However, if you're a woman who covets shoes like Imelda Marcos, you have Zappos on speed-dial. Delivering happiness is a quaint, charming idea, but what Zappos mainly delivers are huge equity positions for the principals and investors, and shoes. And let's face it, what red-blooded female can resist spending ridiculous amounts of money on poorly made, uncomfortable footwear?

To give you some perspective, Zappos was sold to Amazon for over a billion dollars. Yeah, that's the one with nine zeros after it, and nine zeros can deliver a tremendous amount of happiness. *Delivering Happiness* is primarily about how they sold the company for over a billion dollars, but that's not what you'll read on the dust jacket or in any of the myriad blurbs written by some of the world's best-known blurb writers. The book is a scrambled mix of California, touchy-feely hip and B.F. Skinner's *Walden Two.* Inspired by Thoreau's *Walden*, *Walden Two* is the story of a utopian society where everybody works harmoniously toward the common good, and in the case of Zappos, the common good apparently had nine zeros after it.

This is *Miracle on 34th Street* meets *Lion King*. In *Miracle on 34th Street*, as you may recall, Macy's employees send customers to Gimbels, their arch rival, to find merchandise Macy's doesn't have, which is something Hsieh says they do at Zappos. *Lion King* is a society built around the circle of life, cooperative and supportive, living under the benevolent rule and protection of the lions, who every once in a while eat one of their subjects. Hsieh writes *ad nauseum* about what a family Zappos is and how all the Munchkins dance and sing all day long, until of course, it becomes expedient to jettison some of the family for the common good. When was the last time you laid off one of your kids because things got tight? Look, anybody who tells you a company is a family is committing snake-oil-salesmanship to the highest degree. Your family is your family and your job is your job. Hsieh does an admirable job trying to sell the concept that Zappos' layoffs were humane and sensitive, but anyway you dress it up, and regardless of how much money you throw at the victims, you are messing with people's lives with potentially disastrous results, and you are certainly not treating them like family members.

With all its problems and deceptiveness, however, I still enjoyed the book. Hsieh is a relatively interesting character, and some of his ideas are intriguing. One concept he writes about that I really like is something they call PEC, or Personal Emotional Connection. He says

Zappos demands that their employees make a personal emotional connection with their customers, because (now be honest) how satisfying can it be buying a pair of do-me pumps without first encountering a personal emotional connection?

Okay, I'm being facetious and unfair because I believe the concept is solid and valuable. I've written before about the need to connect with your clients and customers in order to fulfill your responsibilities as a professional salesperson, so I'm in full agreement with Hsieh on this subject. Make the customer feel important, because she is. You can't fake it and pretend; that disguise is easily seen through. You have to find within yourself the spot that allows you to open up enough to show care and empathy. That's a huge subject, but a concept worth working on every day.

Unlike Blake in *Glengary Glen Ross*, who never gave a thought to anybody he ever hustled into buying swampland in Florida while sitting in their dining room eating crumb cake. He measured his life in what he saw as material rewards, his BMW and Rolex, but they weren't rewards at all. They were substitutes for real value, the value you get from caring about people and helping them. So instead of ABC standing for always be closing, let's change it around. How about A-B-C. A-Always, B-Be, C-Caring.

Always be caring. That's the real ticket to delivering happiness, not only to your customers, but to yourself.

Six Degrees of Separation

First and foremost, Steve Jobs was a salesman. A great salesman.

In case you live in a cave, cut off from all human contact (a place Jobs tried desperately to create for all of us, metaphorically speaking), Jobs died not too long ago after a long struggle against cancer. The modern media fell all over each other in tributes and retrospectives of the gadget king of supreme alienation. All the cable trash outlets led with his obituary and dedicated hours of sycophantic perturbation. He made the front page of many large-circulation newspapers and appeared on several national magazine covers, including *Time,* where he was deified as one of the greatest men of our times.

The modern media can most definitely get it on.

Just in case you're still listening to music on a Victrola and looking things up in the *World Book Encyclopedia*, Steve Jobs helped usher in the world of instant information and easy access distractions. He was a master at aping technology and brilliantly packaging and selling his moderately innovative products to the identity-starved, great unwashed, who could barely afford the price, but continued to shell out a huge premium to be part of the now generation. And they usually had to stand in line for hours, sometimes all night, to do so. This guy was Harold Hill in a red band frock with shiny buttons and gold shoulder braids, marching down Main Street, USA, enticing and inviting you to join the world of instant electronic gratification. A life of perceived cool was only a swipe away, so fire up those interest-exploding credit cards and damn the exponentially growing balances and *full speed ahead Mr. Boatswain, full speed ahead.*

If you've ever driven two hours to a youth hockey game with your son sitting next to you in the front seat listening to his iPod and navigating the world through his iPhone, you know what I'm talking about. Countless hours and countless money and all I get is an occasional grunt if I dare to break the sacred dance of Facebook braying.

Goodbye, Mr. Jobs. You did a fine job.

But you did create excitement. Always. And in the most removed, six-degrees-of-separation way, I got to touch that sacred cloth of cool for a nanosecond. That was in 1984, not too long after the *1984* commercial for the new Macintosh computer, introduced by Apple, was broadcast. It was one of the most expensive TV commercials ever produced until that time, but it only ran once, officially, during the wild-card, overachieving Los Angeles Raiders torpedoing of the unsinkable Washington Redskins in Super Bowl XVIII.

In January 1984, there were two things Americans were looking forward to: the heavily favored Redskins inevitable crowing as champs, and the showing of the much-anticipated Apple Macintosh commercial.

Full speed ahead Mr. Boatswain, full speed ahead.

The game didn't live up to the hype; the commercial did.

Big time.

Certainly one of the most famous commercials of all time, it also happened to work.

Big time.

It did what a commercial is supposed to do: it created a Unique Selling Proposition (UPS), and guess what—it sold product.

Big time.

The concept of the commercial was based on George Orwell's novel *1984*, where the world has slid into a dystopian future ruled by a televised "Big Brother," who represents IBM in the commercial. It was a triumph of style and substance and ranks at the top of my list of greatest commercials. It blew me away then and still does today. Who wouldn't want to jump on that hyper-speed train and ride the revolution? Up against the wall, mother fornicators, and all that other swell 1960-leftover paranoid hyperbole.

And I was all in, baby. Sort of.

In spite of the emotional bloodletting, I kept using my IBM because when all was said and done, I thought Macs were for sissies.

You had to be tough to use Microsoft-based products, and I was all of that.

But the commercial did influence millions to buy into Jobs' vision, and Apple became a formidable opponent to Big Blue in the PC business, and they pretty much did it on the strength of that overwhelmingly effective commercial.

So when I flew to Los Angeles a few months later to meet with the good folks at Chiet Day, the *über* hip advertising agency *du jour* (the agency of record for Apple in those callow days of electronic enlightenment), the aftershock of the *1984* commercial was still very much alive and permeated the entire advertising industry with a red hot buzz, especially in California. I was calling on Chiet Day to introduce a concept for advertising Nike on vertical billboards. They loved the concept and Nike loved the concept, and we worked on its execution for months, but it never took flight. Internal inventory problems at Nike killed the project, along with a good part of their ad budget in the fourth quarter of 1984, but I never felt like I lost on that one. Indeed, I got to hang out in the holy temple and work at ground zero for a moment in time, and be part of the good vibrations of something truly monumental and historic.

Talk about a buzz.

And that's what Steve Jobs was all about. Buzz. Nobody was better at creating excitement and sizzle, and as a result, the man could flat-out sell product. Most people would not have thought of him as a salesman, but that's what he was—a great salesman.

Light Up Your Face with Gladness

It was a busy Saturday morning and I was late. After running errands all over God's green earth, I was on my way to the post office where I had to be by one o'clock. I had to be there by one o'clock because the post office closes at one o'clock on Saturday.

Enjoy it while it lasts.

Why we're still in the mail delivery business on any day of the week is a mystery to me. We've progressed past the needs of our pioneering heritage when it was a genuine challenge and adventure to post a missive from one place to another. It shouldn't take a logistical genius like Benjamin Franklin to figure out that neither snow nor rain nor heat nor gloom of night stays the brave new world of 4G hyper-communications. And in our modern incarnation of long-distance social intercourse, you don't have to worry about dealing with the unpredictable and harsh elements, getting attacked by an opponent of manifest destiny, or being eaten by lions and tigers and bears, oh my.

Anachronism or not, that's where I was heading on a Saturday morning, and by almost one o'clock in the afternoon I hadn't eaten all day. So I did what the average, busy, overloaded American usually does in such a situation—I pulled into a fast-food emporium of empty calories and simple carbs.

The horror, the horror!

I don't normally eat fast foods, but my stomach was growling and the last ding-dong of doom was ringing at my local post office. This particular fast-food joint is located across the highway from a large amusement park and the place was jammed on this hot summer weekend with the drive-through backed up and snaking around the parking lot. I decided it would be quicker to run inside, grab a quick burger and roll on down the road. But the inside was just as congested as the parking lot. People were all over the place, and dozens of employees were running hither and yon, some with bags of close facsimiles of hot foodstuffs, others snatching the moolah from the eager hands of the hopeful lost souls salivating like Pavlov's dog, waiting for the bell that tolls for them.

And nobody was smiling.

The employees were polite and efficient, but never made eye contact or acknowledged your presence other than performing their duties.

After patiently waiting in line, I placed my order and joined the frozen-in-time tapestry of suspended vessels of arteries about to be hardened.

I waited.

And I waited.

And I waited.

And then I didn't wait anymore. I went up to one of the overworked employees and asked for my money back. With no acknowledgement that she had even heard me, she took my receipt, went to the food bins, grabbed two burgers, threw them in a bag, went to the cash register, counted out some money, then came back to me with the burgers and my money.

"You don't have to give me my money back if I'm getting my order," I said.

"You asked for your money back, didn't you?" she replied and rushed away.

Wow. I was stunned. I had only ordered one burger, but I got two and my money back. And guess what, I felt guilty as hell. It was an uncomfortable experience, and although the employee had shown great diplomacy and had gone the distance to take care of me, she left me feeling pretty bad, and as I drove out of the parking lot I made a mental note not to return, ever.

When I had time to think about the experience and evaluate why I had reacted the way I did, I came to understand that the employees had done their job extremely well under the circumstances, but they had lost sight of why they were doing it. Although they obviously didn't realize it, their job was to make people feel good about doing business with them, and on that count they had failed. They failed because they didn't give the simplest, easiest gift one person can give to another—a smile.

For years I have being teaching salespeople that the most effective tool they can use on a sales call is their smile. It makes the client feel good, and you know what? It makes you feel good, too. If the employees of the fast food restaurant had added a smile to their already efficient process, I would have felt better. Actually, I probably would have felt great, but instead I felt like I had done something wrong and left the place in some pain.

All that good work for nothing and it could have been avoided with a natural, effortless smile. Remember, if you smile at someone, they just might smile back, and who knows what that might lead to.

Incidentally, everybody at the post office smiled at me, and I left there that day feeling terrific and thinking maybe we should keep the old place around a while longer.

See De Pyramids Along De Nile

Welcome to the Hotel California...

...where, according to the Eagles' 1976 hit, "Hotel California," they haven't had wine since 1969, but they keep pink champagne on ice.

Huh?

The problem is that champagne is wine. Sorry to be pedantic, but I'm sure a few of you didn't know that. After all, some people don't seem to know much because here we are back in the 1970s with bellbottoms, hip huggers and platform shoes, now considered *haute couture,* but without a doubt the most unbecoming clothing ever worn by women, almost as bad as skinny jeans on men. So what we have here is an enigma wrapped in a paradox surrounded by overwrought songwriting, replete with metaphors gone wild.

Which brings me to multi-level marketing, or as it is known in the trade, MLM. These types of businesses also use the names Home Based Business, Direct Marketing, Network Marketing, Relationship

Marketing, and the more accurate description (for my money, anyway), Pyramid Marketing. But you'll be hard pressed to find anybody in the industry who uses the word "pyramid."

"Yeah, you're gonna make a fortune just by gettin' teams of salespeople under you, and teams of salespeople under them, and teams of salespeople under them, and so on and so forth. But this is no pyramid. No siree, Bob! Just take a little sip of this here Kool-Aid and while you're at it, get your friends and family to take a little sip too and you'll soon be wearing a smiley face and be-bopping on down the highway paved with bright, shiny gold."

Unfortunately for MLM businesses, almost everything you hear or read that doesn't come from within the industry is negative, and generally well earned. Let's face it, many of these businesses are nothing more than loosely constructed, fly-by-night schemes to milk all they can from the pump of high hopes and low prospects until the last trickle of rust is all that's left. And in these economically challenging times, promise and hope are marketable commodities: "Just sign on the dotted line and let's get this trivial matter of the small deposit of $4,999 for your sales kit out of the way. Remember, you get a nice percentage of each deposit for every guppy, er, prospect you sign up, and another percentage for every sucker, make that associate, they rope, I mean bring in, and you can see it won't take long to recoup your money and make tons more."

MLM companies seem to be proliferating during the current economic crisis, and the more I see, the more I'm convinced most are nothing more than con jobs fleecing desperate people looking for opportunities. Look, not all MLM companies are disreputable and dishonest, but the truth is, most of them are designed to make the people at the top rich. The basic principle is that the top draws from the bottom, and that revenue stream is only as healthy as the organization's ability to recruit new members. What generally happens, however, is that the folks on the lower levels make little money and, more often than not, end up losing money. It's really a question of where you are on the pyramid, and the viability of the pyramid's structure.

There are some simple questions to ask before getting involved in an MLM, but the most basic one is, does the product have value, and if so, why isn't it being sold like all other products using time-tested marketing and merchandising methods? Is the market for this product so competitive or so oversaturated or the product too weak and marginal to survive in an aggressive marketplace? Is the product only a thin veil to hide an exploitative pyramid scheme? Also, you might want to ask if you will make most of your money selling product or by recruiting friends and neighbors.

In spite of all the problems, MLM companies are making money, lots of money. According to *Direct Selling News*, in 2010, direct-selling companies generated over $125 billion in revenue in 150 countries by 75 million reps. Some of the more well-known MLM companies are Avon, Herbalife, Mary Kay and Amway, and they've all been around a long time and many people have earned a great deal of money from them, not to mention a few pink Cadillacs along the way. My mom used to buy Avon products when I was a kid, and my first deodorant was Avon, and I've purchased Herbalife vitamins over the years. Additionally, I know several reputable, professional salespeople heavily involved in MLM groups who are happy and making a good living.

The problem is, these companies are run pretty much like casinos. Casinos know a few people will win big, but they also know that the vast majority of gamblers will lose, and those losses fund the big winners who help promote the concept to new and naive players, drooling over the grand possibilities. Like playing the slots or blackjack, getting involved in an MLM company can be risky. And then there's the cult-like ambiance of the serenely proselytized whispering in your ear over and over again, *you can check out any time you like, but you can never leave.*

What Is a Salesman

In movies, TV shows, commercials, theater and other media, salespeople are usually portrayed as cheats and liars. That's our sad lot in life: to be viewed in the most negative ways, to be the bad guy, never to wear the white hat and ride off into the sunset with the orchestra playing a heart-thumping, emotional tribute to the conquering hero. Generally, we slither off somewhere before the final act.

Every day we go forth to fight the good fight, dragging along behind us the reputation of age-old snake oil peddlers selling magic elixir and can't-miss remedies to all our problems, thump, thump, thump, always there like an anvil chained to our ankle. We are, without a doubt, part of a painfully misunderstood profession. Oh yes, there are disingenuous cheats and liars out there selling used cars with sawdust in the transmission or convoluted Ponzi schemes, but most salespeople are honest, hard-working folk who have a great deal of pride and integrity.

Years ago—I don't remember when or where—somebody gave me this description of a salesperson (before we started using more gender sensitive nomenclature). I've always enjoyed it because I think it's the most accurate depiction of what it's really like to carry a bag and pound the pavement to earn your daily bread.

What Is a Salesman?

A salesman is a pin on a map to the sales manager, a quote to the factory, an overloaded expense account to the auditor, a bookkeeping item called "cost-of-selling" to the treasurer, a smile and a wisecrack to the receptionist and a purveyor of flattery to the buyer.

A salesman needs the endurance of Hercules, the brass of Barnum, the craft of Machiavelli, the tact of a diplomat, the tongue of an orator, the charm of a playboy and the brain of a computer.

He must be impervious to insult, indifference, anger, scorn, complaint and be razor-sharp even after drinking until dawn with a customer.

He must have the stamina to sell all day, entertain all evening, drive all night to the next town and be on the job fresh at 9:00 a.m.

He must be good at storytelling and willing to lose at golf and cards.

He wishes his merchandise was better, his prices lower, his commissions higher, his territory smaller, his competitors more ethical, his goods more promptly delivered, his boss more sympathetic, his advertising more effective and his customers more human.

But he is a realist who accepts the fact that none of this will ever be. He lives or dies by the daily report.

He rolls his days away in the tedium of planes, trains and automobiles. He sleeps his nights away in cheerless hotel rooms.

Each morning he hoists onto his back the dead weight of last year's quota and goes forth to do it all over again.

Yet, for all that, he is absolutely certain that tomorrow will be better and there is nothing he would rather do, or anybody he would rather be, than a salesman.

That still gives me a chill. Maybe I'm too sentimental or stubbornly maintain an overblown, romantic vision of sales, but I'm sure of one thing: There is absolutely nothing I would rather do, or anybody I would rather be, than a salesman.

Take the Money and Run

Apparently, some people think I hate sales trainers. They think I have no respect for their contribution to the art of selling, and that they are primarily in it to take the money and run, regardless of what tripe they have to sell to get it.

No way Jose; in fact, quite the contrary. One of the most positive influences in my life was my first sales trainer. He taught me more about myself and life in three weeks than I had learned up to that point in my short but relatively eventful existence on this green, semi-round orb. I've run into some other trainers over the years I thought were pretty good, too. Not to mention that I've done quite bit of sales training myself.

So to say I hate sales trainers would be a gross overstatement. A truer statement would be that I think many of them are fakes, charlatans and snake oil salesmen, hiding behind the curtain and controlling the smoke and illusions. Over the years, I have often compared sales trainers and motivational speakers to a summer job I had in high school.

I was a laborer on a crew building fences. Every morning the foreman would line up the holes for the fence posts and start digging them with a gas-powered post-hole digger. In every hole, at some point, he would hit a rock, or multiple rocks, and my job was to use a post-hole digging and tamping bar to get the rocks out. It was hard work, raising the bar high up over my head with both hands and slamming it down repeatedly on the rocks, trying to either move them and pry under them, or smash them into smaller pieces. Every so often, I would grab a shovel and dig out the rocks or pieces of rocks and dirt I had loosened. It was a back-breaking job and probably the most tiring work I have ever done.

The owner of the company would visit our work site a couple times a day, often sitting in his truck and watching us work while drinking a cup of coffee and smoking a cigarette. One day, while I was using the post-hole bar, he jumped out of the truck and hurried over to me, snatching the bar out of my hands. "That's not how you dig a hole," he yelled at me, and he started pounding on the rocks like John Henry going against the steam-powered hammer; then he grabbed the shovel and dug like a crazy man. Finally, after only a few minutes of work, he threw the shovel to the ground in disgust and looked up at me, beads of sweat running down his forehead. "Now that's how you dig a hole," he groused through clenched teeth, and walked back to his truck and proceeded to drink his coffee.

As I stared at the shovel sticking in a pile of soft earth, it occurred to me, "I could do that for a couple of minutes. But how do you work like that all day in the hot sun?" The truth is that you couldn't. Nobody could, although the owner of the fence company would have me believe that's how I should be working. In reality, I had to pace myself; I had to ration my strength and stamina to get through the whole day, not just a short demonstration.

The owner of the fence company tried to make me feel guilty; that was his idea of motivation. And that's what most trainers, coaches and motivational gurus do. They're great in the short run, but where are they when you've had your head handed to you by three customers in a row and you feel like taking a long walk off a short pier? They're flying to their next engagement in their own private jet.

Maybe you think that's a bit cynical, and maybe it is, but those opinions were forged over years of reading, watching and studying the so-called experts in the field. Most of what I've seen is nothing more than rehashed, repackaged pablum aimed at making an extremely complicated and always moving, always changing subject simple and easy to swallow. You know—do this and say that and get rich. Bada bing!

The other problem I have with these guides to our innermost dreams and aspirations is that their agendas are usually built around keeping customers coming back for more, which means they aren't really trying to fix anything or help people become more competent and independent. Just the opposite, actually. They want their minions to be dependent on them so they can keep milking the cow for free, without having to do any of the real work that goes into housing, feeding and keeping the cow comfortable and happy enough to continue producing milk. In other words, many of them are takers, not givers, although they would have you believe just the opposite.

Just like some therapists who get rich off other people's pain and sorrow, the last thing they want is for their golden goose to get better. What, are you kidding? And turn off the tap that bought him a yacht and sent his kids to expensive colleges? The game is to make people think you're helping them while making them even more dependent on you, which takes some real talent—and an empty soul. In order to be effective at this kind of deception, you need to zero in on a person's needs and vulnerabilities and exploit them mercilessly. I once observed a trainer position himself as a saleswoman's only friend against her company and her boss, and for those of us who have been pounding the pavement long enough, we know how susceptible we can be to those kinds of weak moments. We're all subject to distractions and excuses from time to time, and with the right kind of stimulus and support, those temporary problems can be turned into a poison, a poison for which your good friend the sales trainer holds the only antidote. And the salesperson's boss, the guy who ends up holding the sticky end of the wicket, foots the bill. It's a beautiful thing in the hands of a master, if you happen to be a fan of depravity and sadism.

On the other hand, I believe in solid, fundamental sales training, and I believe it should be an ongoing, progressive process. Its purpose should be to straighten and support, not to rebuke and tear down. But that's a subject for another time. Until then, however, there are two people you can read and study if you want some valuable, helpful advice. The first is Dale Carnegie. *How to Win Friends and Influence People* is 75 years old, but it's still the best book of advice for salespeople and pretty much the basis for almost everything written about selling since. The underlying tenet is that you need to listen to people in order to understand them and gain their trust. The other guy is Zig Ziglar. He's an old timer, too, but truth is eternal, and one of his basic truths is that if you want to be successful, you have to care about people.

There it is, the simple, easy-to-use truth about sales. Listen and care. Now you know everything you need to know to be a success, and it didn't cost you a dime (other than the infinitesimally small pittance you paid for this invaluable tome of definitive knowledge). By no means do I buy into everything Dale Carnegie and Zig Ziglar believe and espouse, and I disagree with them on some points, but these two simple principles will set you free and send you to the head of your sales group.

Okay, so now you know what to do, but not how to do it. That is what good sales training is all about, and it can't be answered in a short bromide or three-hour session. Learning how to use these truths is a lifetime pursuit and what makes selling such a wonderful, rewarding experience. Ziglar compares sales training to bathing: You have to keep doing it if you want to stay clean, and if you're like me, you probably fall in the mud once in a while. When you do, nothing feels better than a long, hot shower.

So keep bathing, my friends, and remember: Oz is no more of a wizard than you are.

Crisis of Faith

Wikipedia describes crisis of faith as "a term commonly applied to periods of intense doubt and internal conflict about one's preconceived beliefs or life decisions. A crisis of faith can be contrasted to simply a period of doubt in that a crisis of faith demands reconciliation or reevaluation before one can continue believing in whichever tenet is in doubt or continuing in whatever life path is in question."

Crisis of faith.

Man, do we of the small but confident band of the initiated souls of the forever-shifting brotherhood of drummers, canvassers and knockers battle that demon. Probably more than any other profession, our beliefs and life decisions are called into question on a fairly regular basis, mainly because our ability, our performance and our character are judged on a daily basis. And in sales, those judgments are almost always negative and intended to make us feel guilty and unworthy, the idea being that we will work even harder in order to correct those shortcomings.

Unfortunately, in practice it seldom works that way. The usual result of that type of critical management style is feeling badly about your performance and the job itself. And when it's served up piping hot on a daily basis, you start to question your own self-worth. Ergo, a crisis of faith.

We all go through them—the young, the not-so-young, the inexperienced, the veterans, anybody who's ever worn the yoke of last year's numbers and who gets up every morning to sally forth one more time into the cave of the fire-breathing dragon. If you're in sales and you haven't experienced periods of melancholy and self-doubt, then you're not doing it right. Good salespeople are driven more by pride and competiveness than money or other material rewards (although that's the medium by which we usually judge our victories and defeats), and when we are reminded incessantly of our perceived (manufactured?) failures, we react emotionally. Painfully emotionally.

Even awards, prizes and trips serve to do more negative damage to the psyche of the group than any positive reinforcement within the few. The many receive nothing of affirmation, only the sharp recognition of more failure, while the winners are feted and praised for a short period of time, then thrown right back in the systemic stew of what-have-you-done-for-us-lately. Acknowledgment in sales is a bittersweet apple to bite into, and the aftertaste can spoil your palate in a downward spiral of an ego-gratification-meets-reality hangover.

The Romans had it right. Generals and emperors who had won a great victory, when returning home would take part in a triumphal procession through the city's streets. In the procession were slaves and captives, carts loaded with plunder and ranks of marching soldiers and cavalry. During the parade, a slave stood in the chariot behind the victorious general and over the general's head held a garland of laurel, signifying victory. As the procession moved through the streets of ancient Rome, the slave would repeatedly whisper in the general's ear, "All glory is fleeting. All glory is fleeting."

All glory is fleeting!

Ask any salesperson who's been around a while how true that short statement is. The good news is that although glory is fleeting, so is pain, at least the kind spooned out in the daily grub line of hit-your-quota, Bub, if you want more gruel slapped on your plate at tomorrow's offering. The problem is, it takes a great deal of hard work and self-discipline to work through the debilitating pain of uncertainty and get back to the glory days, an ability prevalent in successful salespeople. When good trainers and managers talk about having to work hard to be successful, they're not simply talking about putting in time as much as they are talking about the mental toughness of staying ever vigilant against the demon of sales despair; it's about the reconstruction process we go through periodically to reinforce and strengthen our resolve and commitment.

It's about gutting it out. You get tough or you perish. End of story.

And that's what makes sales so great, at least for me: the constant struggle between the power of a dark and bitter force against the strength of a validating and liberating spirit. Like the Charlie Sheen character in the movie *Platoon*, whose soul is torn between the malevolent Sergeant Barns (played by Tom Berringer) and the empowering Sergeant Elias (played by Willem Dafoe), a salesperson's soul is in an ongoing battle between colliding perspectives.

It's easy, and sometimes necessary, to take a walk on the dark side. Sales is a tough, lonesome job, with lots of problems and negative distractions, and it's almost impossible to run that gauntlet on a daily basis without getting some of the slime on you. And when the slime starts to mount up to a point where you need a straw to breathe, it's time to get to work, once again, on reconciling and reevaluating your belief in the most basic of all tenets, your own self-worth. It really is a simple question of faith, and when that faith is tainted or challenged, when you have trouble believing in who you are and what you do, when you fight through the tangle and undergrowth and burst out into bright, shining sunlight, you are one step closer to being a better salesperson. Good salespeople, like good marriages, are not the ones who never have to face any problems, they're the ones that work through the problems.

As much as I hate clever bromides and platitudes, there are a couple I particularly like. The first is that my life will not be defined by what is wrong, but by what is right. The second is that I will not be judged by the number of times I get knocked down, but by the number of times I get up.

Getting up is really what it's all about; it defines who we are. So don't worry about getting knocked down. Just keep getting up.

And keep the faith.

Hard Times, Part 1

Happy Valentine's Day.

I wish I could send a dozen, long-stemmed red roses to all the girls I've known before, but who can afford it? At 35 bucks a pop, the cost of repentance-flavored nostalgia is much too high. I used to pay $70 on Lupercalia in the olden days of easy money, before the harsh reality of accounts payable rose its ugly head and we all started surveying the local gas stations for the cheapest prices. Back in those halcyon days of wine and roses, who even knew what a gallon of gasoline cost?

That was before we all had to have a giant, super-duper, mega grocery store within a mile or two of our homes; one of those ultra-hip, modern marketplaces complete with chic cafe attached to a food court, fish market, sushi bar, butcher shop, pharmacy, liquor store, beer distributor, notions emporium, and, of course, a florist. That was back when a dozen roses cost around $40, except on or about February 14, when the price skyrocketed simply because the market could and would bear it. Now you pay about $10 a dozen at the new crossroads of America, but they, too, jack up the price on the one day of the year when money seems to be of no object when it comes to the thorny business of mass-marketed love, or close facsimiles thereof.

It's not the $30 that bothers me; I mean who cares about dropping that pittance on a bunch of prickly South American flora that in short order will drop dried-up petals and runaway baby breath blooms all over your place, before the charge even hits your credit card account? No, what bothers me is that I pay $10 the rest of the year. For years the independent florists educated me that they can sell a dozen roses for $40 and make a nice profit, but on Valentine's Day, they can make a heck of a lot more. They would justify it by saying the costs of procuring, shipping and distributing roses increased greatly because of the huge demand. Gee, when I was in school studying supply and demand, we were taught that the price of goods went down with increased demand because of greater, more efficient synergies.

Ah, the new math!

So here I am again, the pathetic consumer, paying almost $4 dollars for a gallon of gas for no discernable, logical reason, other than the fact that the oil companies can get away with it. Of course they blame OPEC, but have you seen their earning statements lately? Like the flower industry, they think we're a bunch of gullible, trusting idiots who will step in line and walk peacefully over the edge of all reason and understanding, like a slice of smiling, dunderheaded lemmings.

If the auto industry is any indicator, however, we are finally getting a bit smarter. Owners of car dealerships complain that the average consumer researches cars and prices on the Internet, so by the time they get to the dealership, they know exactly what they will have to pay for a car. Accordingly, the profit margin for new car sales has dropped considerably over the last decade.

My, my.

I wonder when people got the idea they were being fleeced by Detroit to the point where they started educating themselves? Obviously, the Internet gave consumers the means to do so, but do you think the motivation could have sprung from multiple thousand-dollar rebates, zero percent interest rates and no down payments or closing costs? Do you think the auto industry taught people that they were making so much money that they could appear to practically give cars away?

Duh!

But don't be so smug. *We few, we happy few* who earn our daily bread trying to get strangers to give us their money are doing the same thing right now. Selling in this challenging economic climate is hard, real hard, and our customers are demanding more and more from us, especially in the area of price. Whereas price used to be a significant but less than central part of most sales calls, today it dominates the conversation.

That's happening for two reasons. The first is that times are tough, tougher by far than I've seen in the past. Most of us have gone through periods of soft markets before, but they usually were of the roller-coaster variety associated with the predictable ups and downs of a growing, aggressive economy. But this one is different. This one is protracted and seemingly in a degrading pattern where selling continues to get more difficult, not less, as in other recessions and market corrections. Every day we look down the long, dark abyss of the tunnel we're navigating, hoping to see a faint light, indicating the end of this arduous journey. But like the old saying, don't be surprised if that faint light just around the corner is actually the proverbial train coming at us, furnace blasting, steel wheels rumbling along at full speed.

"Casey Jones you better watch your speed. Trouble ahead, trouble behind, and you know that notion just crossed my mind," as the Grateful Dead put it.

The second reason is that, like the auto industry, we have educated our customers to the fact that we can and will, indeed, lower our prices, and once you do that, it's damn near impossible to get the toothpaste back in the tube. Price is always a difficult subject, but there are ways to deal with it, even in these thorny times, without destroying the value of your product or your own credibility.

We'll get into that later. Until then, remember there is probably more opportunity out there in bad times than in good times. The kicker is that you have to be a pretty good salesperson to harvest those gold nuggets. In times like these, only the strong survive, and not only that, they can often flourish.

Hard Times, Part 2

When Davy Jones of the 1960s *The Monkees* TV show died, *People* magazine put him on the cover. I'm guessing he's the first Monkee who made the cover of any major publication since the short-lived show belched forth the ersatz rock group, a Hollywood-manufactured American offering of the British invasion bands sweeping the nation at the time. The Monkees were a meteoric sensation better known for what they couldn't do, like write music or play instruments. However, they worked hard to overcome that image and produced a few hits on their own before the light dimmed and was finally extinguished by the onslaught of the schizoid sounds of the 70s.

People, unconscionably and right there on the cover, in their most over-the-top-and-beyond style, proclaimed Jones as "the man whose fame changed music forever."

Excuse me?

Was anybody at *People* even alive when the Monkees were pretending to be rock stars? Can anyone associated with Henry Luce's worst nightmare possibly justify with any empirical or even whimsical evidence that Davy Jones and the Monkees were ever more than a momentary blip on the radar screen of sex, drugs and rock 'n roll?

My God, man, is anybody paying attention?

Look, they were fun and energetic and I enjoyed their antics and high-strung music back when Elvis was stepping down as king and Buddy Holly was all but forgotten, but let's try to maintain some perspective here.

Unfortunately, it only gets worse. *People* goes on to refer to Jones as "the cute one." As everybody who ever swung a hula hoop or played with a Howdy Doody puppet can attest, the "cute one" was Paul McCartney of the Beatles, the one and only "cute one." There could never be another "cute one," and although the diminutive Jones was pleasantly youthful looking, he falls into the category of flash-in-the-pan-cute with fellow TV phenoms David Cassidy of *The Partridge Family* and Barry Williams from *The Brady Bunch.* To label Jones as "the cute one" is a sacrilege of the highest order.

And business as usual in the world we inhabit today.

Hyperbole and the manipulation of reality are standard fare in today's media smorgasbord of 24/7 cable news, blogs, Facebook and Twitter. Responsible, objective journalism is an anachronism hard to find in these days of you're either "wit us or agin us." Responsible discourse has given way to ham-handed, opinionated oratory in the public dialogue, and since we seem to be either too lazy, too stupid or too indifferent to care about truth, justice and the American way any longer, our judgments and attitudes are shaped and molded by the loudest, most repetitive voices. We seem to have lost our ability or desire to question the absurdities laid before us, and the result is, *voilà*, Davy Jones, "the man whose fame changed music forever."

Gag me with a spoon.

Please.

And then along comes the worst economy since the Great Depression.

As you may have heard, some people believe the media, in general, is governed by left-wing, Eastern elitists who prefer to experience the width and breadth of America from 30,000 feet. These folks, it is rumored, manipulate the news to fit their liberal agendas, and it is further postulated that this unchecked bias can not only influence and even create public opinion, but can actually change reality, if you believe the blowhards on the other side.

The most recent and dramatic example, the right-siders suggest, is the sudden and definitive deconstruction of the economy right before the election of 2008. And when we were approaching the 2012 election, the usual suspects were out trumpeting a phantom recovery. They kept telling us things were getting better, and the other side kept telling us they weren't, but regardless of how it affected the great unwashed (us), all the folks flapping their gums and pounding their keyboards were making millions.

At our expense.

And they want to keep making millions at our expense, so they keep pushing their garbage, and they keep going to the bank.

Meanwhile, back in reality, we of the lesser demographic group (those not making millions) are scratching our heads and wondering WTF.

My advice is to stop listening to that band of narcissists who wouldn't know hard times if they bit them in the ass. Use your own judgment based on your real life experience to form your own opinions, and don't be fooled by the serpents in the garden handing out free apples. And if you happen to be a fellow traveler in the wonderful world of sales, keep your head down.

I'm out on the street every day trying to peddle my goods, and I'm still being bombarded with the pain and fear of an extremely weak economy. I'm critically aware of all the noise about the recovery, but I don't see it yet, so I'm still fighting the good fight against the fire-breathing dragon, still presenting an irresistible force against an unmovable object. And I'm returning home from the crusade every day, bloodied and wounded, but not defeated because I am, after all, a daydream believer looking for that elusive homecoming queen.

Hard Times, Part 3

I've never learned anything in my life from things that came easily. No, I've earned my stripes (as we all have) from my frequent visits to the free clinic of pain and frustration that gleefully accompany challenge and failure. That's where I've found the worthwhile knowledge and experience that moved me forward and created the enormous excitement of accomplishment that gets me up in the morning.

That being the case, we find ourselves presently in the midst of a veritable treasure trove of potential for growth as we paddle like hell against the swelling tide of economic challenges not seen since the Great Depression, fighting against being washed ashore along with the obliterated hopes and dreams of the misfortunate multitude of the mangled masses. That's right, lots of opportunity out there for the hale and hearty, depending on your chosen point of view, of course. After all, one man's ceiling is, indeed, another man's floor, or as

Shakespeare put it, "There is nothing either good or bad, but thinking makes it so."

Epic economic tsunami or field of dreams, it's your call. I have one of those simplistic, inspirational illustrations in my offices, depicting the seventh hole at Pebble Beach, "the most famous little hole in golf," according to *Golf Digest*. The caption reads: *Whether you think you can, or whether you think you can't, you're right.* Now look, I can stand in front of the Empire State Building from now until the 12th of never believing I can leap that famously tall building in a single bound, but no way, no how, not in this lifetime anyway. But when it comes to overcoming preconceived, self-imposed limitations and mental barriers, I think it's pretty accurate.

If there's one thing we've already learned here in the 21st Century, it's that perception is reality.

Really.

No joke.

It may have started out as a joke, at least to those of us unfortunate enough to be the laughed at, but in today's post-communications world of uncensored, undocumented and unbelievable multi-projected barbs of data and opinions, there's no place left to hide—you just can't duck the slings and arrows of outrageous outrage. I mean, Wikipedia has become the number one source of information for most of us former knuckle draggers, and Wikipedia's information, as you may have heard, is by and large submitted by its readers. As a matter of fact, almost anybody can go in and edit information. Some sources claim that the Feds and people who work for the government have been known to change some of the information to make a person look like a good guy or bad guy.

Welcome to the information age.

Uncensored.

Undocumented.

Unbelievable!

So climb aboard and let that modern millennium maelstrom be your umbrella against said slings and arrows of outrageous market conditions. And don't get caught up in what you think is being done to you—do it to yourself. Perceived reality never has been a fixed target; more an evolving concept, pliable and accommodating to the intrepid few who are brave enough to look behind the curtain. In other words, your attitude toward any given situation will always be primary to the eventual outcome. An acquaintance of mine tells a story about him and his young son, who was about four or five years of age at the time, walking through a tough neighborhood of North Philadelphia. My friend had grown up in that neighborhood years before when it was a working class area of neatly kept row homes, but in the years since he had last visited, it had fallen into urban decay. As he and his son were walking down a street of dilapidated homes, many of them boarded up, they were suddenly accosted by three growling, teeth-baring Doberman Pinschers. As my friend froze and squeezed his young son's hand, the dogs surrounded them. My friend was paralyzed with fear, not knowing what to do. His son, however, had a different take on the reality of the situation.

Looking up at his dad and smiling, he said, "I think these dogs like me," and led his dad past the dogs and on down the street.

Remember, there will always be a few Doberman Pinschers standing in your way, growling and showing their teeth, and you can either look on them as a threat and impediment, or just another exciting day in the wonderful world of sales. In my entire career, there have always been those dogs staring me in the face, warning me of the imminent doom waiting around the next corner. I can never remember a time when we weren't in economic peril, when anybody ever said to me, "Boy, these sure are good times we're experiencing. Please let me spend some more money with you."

To show you what I mean, I received a promotional email the other day that opened with the following paragraph: "The field of sales has experienced some dramatic and far-reaching changes over recent years. Today's sales professionals, as well as today's buyers, are better educated, more informed, and have more options than ever before. These changes have created new, exciting and challenging possibilities in every organization. Success requires innovative ideas and finely developed skills."

I also received this message: "We are facing challenging times ahead. As the economy continues to react to market conditions and works to initiate appropriate adjustments and corrections, sales forces in all fields will need to be better prepared, better equipped and better positioned to capitalize on the exciting opportunities this environment of change will create. The new reality of sales is learn to change or be left behind."

Guess when I received that second message—25 years ago!

The more things change, the more things stay the same.

And the same basic principles of selling will get you through our present pecuniary predicament, just as they did 25 years ago.

Hard Times, Part 4

I've written about the Black Horse before, a bar I worked at in New York City back in the early 70s. The place was owned by Jimmy O'Flynn and he had named it in mock tribute to the famous White Horse in Greenwich Village where he and friends had been unceremoniously eighty-sixed one night, much to their inebriated chagrin. The Black Horse was not much more than a simple spirits emporium, unless you consider the assorted and sundry free and not-so-free spirits that floated through the diverse establishment on a fairly regular basis. That cast of characters ran the gamut in those days of identity disillusionment from hippies to cops to Vietnam vets to straight businessmen and, to my primary motivation for floating though, nurses and airline stewardesses (and yes, we called them stewardess then and they didn't get their knickers all bunched up over the perceived indignity of being referred to as what they actually were).

And I met my share of said characters every night and in all manner of configuration (but that's another story for another time). Two of those characters have come to mind lately as we plow through the muck and mire of an economy gone wild. The first is a guy named Wallace who came into the bar irregularly, which fit perfectly well with the irregular environment of the bar. Wallace drank his scotch straight-up and wasn't one for idle chatter. His attraction to the Black Horse was the same as mine, so we had a natural affinity for each other and would often converse about the evening's fare of eligible young tarts (and yes, we called them tarts, and much worse, because back then it was almost mandatory to denigrate women if you were a "real man").

And Wallace was a real man. He was a boatman who worked up and down the coast between New York City and Cape Cod, performing a variety of duties for rich owners of large sailboats. Wallace was a taciturn nomad who suffered no fools, except, for some unknown reason, me. Over several scotches and Marlboros, he would regale me with wonderful stories of his intrepid adventures at sea, and his incredible, fantastic misadventures with the wives and daughters of rich owners of large sailboats. I loved those stories and the time we spent together.

The reason I've been thinking about Wallace lately is because of one of those stories he told me on a cold winter's night in the warm confines of an empty Black Horse, while the rest of the city hunkered down against a raw winter storm howling through the deserted canyons of the Upper East Side of Manhattan. Wallace told me how rich owners of large sailboats liked to use them in the winter, too, so part of his repertoire was to sail the sloops down to Florida in the fall, which meant going around Cape Hatteras on the Outer Banks of North Carolina during the heart of hurricane season. Apparently, the rich owners of large sailboats didn't have the *cojones* to do that themselves. Not only did Wallace have the requisite *cojones*, but he sailed the boats down the east coast alone. No crew or help, just Wallace and a couple bottles of scotch sipping whiskey.

Wallace told how he sailed out of Cape Cod and was making good time until he got about 50 miles north of Hatteras when a storm started kicking up. The closer he got to North Carolina, the worse the storm got. He told me he had sailed through many storms and wasn't particularly concerned until he got to Hatteras and ran into the full fury of a tropical storm with winds up to 70 mph. Wallace was a good seaman and he checked his marine weather monitor regularly. He also was no hero or dummy, and would sail to safe haven if he detected any hint of a large, dangerous storm in his path, but this one sneaked up on him and the National Weather Service, and he was caught in the middle of it with no place to run and hide.

After fighting a protracted losing battle to keep the boat from being broadsided and sunk, his arms aching from the buildup of lactic acid, Wallace finally surrendered to the inevitable, lowered the sails and tied the rudder pointing into the storm. He grabbed a bottle of scotch, went below and tied himself into his bunk. As the boat slammed back and forth with each new offering of Neptune's wrath, and with everything not stowed or secured flying around the small cabin, Wallace laid there singing sea shanties, keeping his mind focused on the next lyric and his next sip of scotch, which by this time were becoming rather prodigious gulps. And by the time the storm passed, Wallace was good and drunk and happy as a lark, singing and dancing back up on deck.

Well, it's been 40 years since I've seen Wallace, but I often think of him and that story, especially lately. I've used Wallace's story during my entire career to help weather the tropical storms and hurricanes of difficult and challenging markets. Whenever I'm faced with seemingly insurmountable obstacles that threaten to scuttle my small vessel in such an enormous sea of fear and debilitating anxiety, good ol' Wallace pops up and I'm back in my bunk, tied in and singing my lungs out.

Allegorically speaking, of course.

In reality, I go back to the safe comfort of the basics and focus on the next step in front of me, blocking out all peripheral distractions that I have no control over.

For many years I have been teaching salespeople a visual image to help them with this concept. I tell them to imagine their job at hand as building a brick wall. If they look at the huge pile of bricks sitting in front of them, the thought of building the wall can be daunting and unmanageable; the concept is too large to deal with in any organized or efficient manner. However, if they focus on laying one brick at a time, and don't worry about the finished wall, before they know it, the wall is built and they're feeling pretty good about themselves.

Brick by brick by brick.

So focus on one brick at a time and don't worry about the wall. Each one of those bricks will take care of the wall for you.

That's what I learned from Wallace. If you're still alive and still chasing the wives and daughters of rich owners of large sailboats, good luck, Wallace, and thanks.

Hard Times, Part 5

I had been hanging around the bar for a couple months, which in those days was an eternity, and I had come to know the eclectic cast of characters that peopled the anomaly known as the Black Horse. In short order I had become a regular. That was not unusual because in those days of daily attitudinal adjustments and fluctuating hemlines, short order was the order of the day. That's about as long as our collective spans of attention could grasp onto any one subject in those turbulent, cascading times before Ritalin and incessantly moving graphics bombarded our limited consciousness while trying to watch a simple-minded football game, before the necessity of showing a comely sideline reporter with large breasts every few minutes to reacquire our fleeting external awareness.

It was a Saturday night and Jimmy O'Flynn always worked the bar on Friday and Saturday nights. They were big nights and he wanted to watch the cash flow in, and not so much out in the pocket of a hired hand. After years of stealing from other bar owners on his journey to buying his own joint, Jimmy had learned all the bartender tricks of the trade for sharing the wealth, and knew just how vulnerable his elusive cash flow could be. His usual night man during the week, Hank, would jump behind the bar on weekends if it got too busy for Jimmy to handle alone, but he was away, so when the place started to percolate on a particularly warm night in May and the sweet, young things' skirts were up to their high and their mighty (where my attention had been riveted for most of the evening), Jimmy looked up at me from his chores of pouring drinks and washing glasses and smiled.

"Let's go," he said, motioning me to come around behind the bar.

He had intimated on a few occasions that he would teach me to bartend, but he had never initiated any real conversation about it. And that made sense. If you were going to do something at the Black Horse, you didn't talk about it, you just did it. And I was a card-carrying member of the curious and questing tribe of extemporaneous samplers of the bittersweet fruits of life and a little thing like not knowing what I was doing would not stand in my way.

So there I was, pouring draft beers and mixing drinks. Jimmy even taught me to make a martini that night, and in the midst of all the noise and the booze and the chaos, I realized bartending was a blast. The hard work aside, it was exciting and you got to be the center of attention, especially to the pretty young ladies who crowded the liquor-stained bar and vied for my attention.

Oh, boy!

And so began my career as a bartender at O'Flynn's Black Horse in New York City in 1970.

One of the menagerie of off-beats and aberrations who made up the complex citizenry of the Black Horse was a fellow by the name of Don Choate. Don was, for all outward appearances, a straitlaced salesman, probably in his early to mid-thirties, but mature and respectable looking, especially next to the rough-hewn cadre of freaks and misfits ensconced in that pre-postmodern den of iniquity. Don wore suits and ties and button-down Oxford shirts, and drove a conservative, four-door company car. How he ended up in the Black Horse became less of a mystery as I got to know him. He was traveling incognito, well-disguised in a nine-to-five world of business and commerce, but a rambunctious good-time-Charlie when the sun went down, fighting the good fight by day, slipping into a miasma of mood enhancers and perspective augmenters by night.

Don was a freak at heart but he looked like Dale Carnegie incarnate. Ironically, I looked like a freak but was Dale Carnegie in waiting. Don somehow saw that in me; he knew where I was going before I did, which was his great gift—he could look into people's souls, or so it appeared, which is why he was such a good salesman. He always wore a friendly, animated smile and uncompromisingly offered a firm, warm handshake to loosen your heart. Don could B.S. with the best of them, and he could pick your pocket while you nodded and smiled a goofy smile of thanks for liberating you from the heavy burden of monetary responsibility.

He was a piece of work extraordinaire.

It was some time after that first night of my relatively short but happy career as a mixologist when Don first snared me with his Technicolor dream-world of reality-camouflaged-as-fantasy. I was working behind the bar while he held sway over a small group of as-yet-to-be-proselytized devotees, entertaining and mesmerizing them with his elaborate and grand images of hope and salvation. It was like watching a small but enthusiastic multitude of truth seekers in the mystic midst of a soul-reawakening papal audience. He was at his best that night, which meant he was blowing more smoke up their *derrières* than Puff the Magic Dragon. He was always blowing smoke up somebody's *derrière* and I guessed it was only a matter of time until some of that smoke drifted my way, like Prufrock's "yellow fog that rubs its back upon the window-panes, the yellow smoke that rubs its muzzle on the window-panes, licked its tongue into the corners of the evening."

When he had finished his sermon with the newly baptized, he turned his guns on me, opening with a big, toothy grin and friendly, disarming salutation. Don and I had become friends by then, but I had yet to experience firsthand his full-throated oratory of charming bombast.

In those times of alienation and self-disenfranchisement, there was no better medium to express your displeasure and anger at the establishment than through music, so I wrote some very bad songs, songs I would sit on the back bar and sing, accompanied by my equally bad guitar playing. Fortunately, the denizen of Jimmy O'Flynn's pleasure parlor were usually experiencing some kind of consciousness altering, so I'm not sure most of them noticed.

Don did.

We talked that night about my music and Don was his usual, overly enthusiastic self, portraying me as the greatest troubadour since Bob Dylan. He was painting pie-in-the-sky pictures and I was enjoying the ride.

"You're a terrific musician and your songs are creative and interesting," he laid out there with his hands smoothing over the rough spots, like a master mason carefully troweling mortar for his next line of bricks. "You could be a great musician and I'm sure you could make a living off your music, but you've got bigger things waiting for you," he offered as he slowly turned the corner.

What could be bigger than half-crazed girls breaking down my door?

"You're going to be a mover and shaker; you're going to be the star maker," and he was off and running now in the direction he had been navigating toward, moving back and forth at the bar, contorting his body with each point, shuffling his feet for emphasis, both hands waving all over the place.

No stopping him now, a runaway train gaining momentum as it rumbles down the tracks.

"Like that first night you went behind the bar," he continued without taking a breath. "Jimmy looks at you and you jump behind the bar, just like that, not a second thought. You've never been behind a bar and you don't know a thing about bartending, but there you go, everybody spreads out of your way like the Red Sea parting for Moses, nobody's going to get in your way. Okay, here we go, not a thought to what you don't know, only what you can do. You turn your attention to the job at hand and everyone can see the exhilaration and delight coming from you. Man, you're in your element, you're in charge, you're the boss."

"What it'll be, bub?"

Don's smiling and waving his hands as he goes on and on about my adventurousness and fearless spirit, how I'm Daniel Boone and Charles Lindbergh and Neil Armstrong all rolled into one. Boy, I'm the cat's meow in Don's eyes, for the moment anyway, and he can't lay it on thick enough.

"You're the captain of the ship," and now we're heading out to sea.

"You're behind the wheel of a big steamer, heading out of New York Harbor, not worried a bit that you've never piloted a ship before. You're at the helm, shouting out orders, full speed ahead," and now he's facing me, feet spread like he's trying to keep his balance against the swift current, both hands on the large, imaginary wheel, eyes fixed on the horizon, and it occurs to me that Don really is driving that ship.

What an incredible showman.

And what an incredible salesman.

He had me that night as he went on and on with one interesting and provocative metaphor after another, and when he was done, I never felt better about myself. Whatever Don saw in me, he fixed his arrow on the spot and delivered a great deal of happiness. He sold me on something I didn't even know I was in the market for: Me.

Don lived by the simple, most basic principle of sales: Always make the other person feel good about him or herself, and he could do that better than anybody I've ever known. He was successful at it not because he created a fantasy for you, but because he would take the time to discover who you really were. He could relate to anybody and truly enjoyed the process, which is the most important attribute a salesperson can possess.

But we'll get into that when I tell you how Don passed a group of us off as the cast from a hit Broadway show.

Hard Times, Conclusion

Most people, from all walks of life, get in trouble because they lose sight of the fundamental truths, especially today in the world of commerce. America used to be the strongest industrial nation in the world because industry was being led by entrepreneurs and visionaries, not a bunch of privileged MBAs and philistine bean counters. Where we used to concentrate on product, for the past 30 years or so we've focused primarily on profit, which, in this case, is like putting a wheelless cart before a broken-down horse. Profits follow the utility and marketability of a product, not the other way around, and although some of our so-called best and brightest have tried to push that rancid lard as a delicacy, we find ourselves in this economic mess as a result of the survival of the weakest; the dweebs and nerds have taken over and the true warriors who built this country have been rendered superfluous and *passé*. Today's leaders would have to jump up a notch or two just to be considered wimps.

Ed Rendell, the former governor of the Commonwealth of Pennsylvania and mayor of Philadelphia, published a book titled *A Nation of Wusses*. Other than his blind loyalty to the Phillies, Flyers, Eagles and Sixers, I don't always agree with the Gov (as he's affectionately known among Philly sports fans), but he absolutely nailed the state of the country.

We have become a bunch of gutless wusses, and throughout history, whenever gutless wusses are in charge, the consequences are usually pretty awful.

So here we are at awful and gaining ground on stinking-to-high-heaven.

Led by an irresponsible, partisan media and protected by an irresponsible, partisan legal system, the fundamental truth we've lost (that has gotten us into this mess) is that making money, in and of itself, doesn't feed the bulldog, at least not the bulldog that chases the cat that runs on the spinning wheel, generating value and self-worth, and since all business and commerce are driven by sales and salespeople, we are in the sour soup along with all the other culprits for the devaluation of fundamental principles and critical integrity. More than most endeavors, sales is a constant struggle to reject the easy way and stay on the course that delivers real value: self-esteem and happiness that come from a sense of accomplishment by helping others.

Don Choate knew that; he was always helping others, and he was never untrue to his values, except once in a while when he had to lie or smudge the truth a bit in order to deliver that help.

Like the time we went to New Hope.

It was a beautiful summer day for the trip Don had eagerly planned. New Hope, Pennsylvania, was, and remains, a small community of artists with numerous and interesting quaint shops and galleries, nestled on the eastern border of picturesque Bucks County, on the banks of the Delaware River. Don had been promoting the trip for a couple of weeks, so six of us packed into his spiffy four-door, Fairlane 500 and headed south. Don wanted to spend the day drinking wine and strolling through the myriad boutiques and stores, with a big finish at the Stockton Inn just outside of Lambertville, New Jersey, across the river from New Hope.

The guy was cuckoo over the Stockton Inn. It had been around since George Washington sported real teeth, and was famous for its wishing well, immortalized in a 1936 Rodgers and Hart song called "There's a Small Hotel," and covered by Frank Sinatra in the movie version of *Pal Joey* in 1957. Don loved Sinatra, who was old and corny to most of us (although that would change over time—I saw him twice, once at the Latin Casino in Cherry Hill, New Jersey, and once in Atlantic City at one of those nondescript casinos). During our hour-long ride that morning, Don would every once in a while break into the song, "There's a small hotel with a wishing well. I wish that we were there together." It turned out to be a fabulous day. It was everything Don wanted it to be and more—we all had a great time, in spite of our trepidations. And, as advertised, we ended up in the courtyard of the Stockton Inn just about sundown, where we waited for a table.

That's when the real fun began.

The inn was a stately structure that spoke of an elegant history and had an unmistakable feel of days gone by, where five hippies from New York City with long hair and tie-dyed attitudes stuck out like a bunch of dandelions in a well-manicured garden. Accordingly, we were politely and with great reverence refused seating.

Anyone else would have been crestfallen and stymied, but not Don. As complex a concept as I've ever encountered, he could be a man for all seasons and rise to any occasion. He was also very bright and could dance with the best of them.

He gave the matronly hostess one of his heart-melting smiles and gently touched her arm. "Excuse me," he said. "I understand completely and do not want to be a bother, but could I please see the manager before we leave?"

A few minutes later, Don was back and we were being escorted to a beautifully appointed table and fussed over like we were visiting royalty. After we ordered our drinks and were alone, someone from our flabbergasted group asked Don what he had told the manager.

"I told him you were from the cast of *Hair* (a huge Broadway hit in 1970).

Being the ever-diligent pragmatist, I couldn't believe it. "Don," I said, "Broadway's not dark tonight. The curtain for *Hair* went up an hour ago. How did you pull that off?"

"I didn't," he said. "They did. You see, like most people, these folks live ordinary lives with little excitement, and everybody wants, what everybody needs, is a little excitement now and then. I simply gave them what they wanted, what they needed, and I helped them feel good about themselves. Look, they weren't going to let you in simply because of the way you look. That would have been a tragedy because it would be placing limits on what they can and can't experience. I just gave them a little push; I simply liberated them to the experience, a real gift if you ask me. Regardless of the illogic of the idea, they will tell people for the rest of their lives that they waited on the cast from *Hair*, and what a delightful experience it was, how wonderful you all were despite the way you looked. And who's to say you guys aren't in *Hair*. I don't know what you do every night," and he laughed at his own dumb joke.

For the rest of the meal, the staff waited on us hand and foot, and everybody in the place stared. We were celebrities in their eyes, and we definitely delivered more excitement than they'd had in quite some time, and to be perfectly honest, we enjoyed it, too.

Don understood that in order to be successful you had to help people, and he was helping the good but misguided folks at the Stockton Inn that night. That's why he could sell—he understood the two basic principles of success: Make people feel good about themselves and help them. If you let those two simple truths be your mantra, you'll transcend any temporary hard times.

It's that simple, like truth always is.

I learned a great deal from Don Choate in those formative years of my enlightenment. It always felt good to be around him, and he was always entertaining. As we left the Stockton Inn on that incredible night, he was singing and dancing down the narrow, stone path.

When the steeple bell
says "Good night sleep well"
we'll thank the small hotel.
We'll creep in our little shell.
And we will thank the small hotel together.

The Price Is Right

I wrote earlier that I would get to the subject of price, but I got waylaid. I wanted to write about price because price is an important theme for most salespeople. It can dominate sales calls and presentations, and, as a matter of fact, I don't think I've ever been on a sales call where price didn't come up as a concern or an objection, to some extent. Even though having to deal with price can give salespeople the heebie-jeebies, there are legitimate situations where a prospect can't afford what you're selling, but hopefully you will have qualified that up front. It's doubly difficult to deal with price if you work for a company that has a history of marking down price at different rates for different customers, or who doesn't maintain the integrity of their pricing structure. But for most of us, it's an issue of having a tenuous perspective regarding the wicked bugaboo that leaves us all shaking in our Buster Browns.

Trainers and sales managers will tell you there are no real price objections, only value objections, and that is almost always true. After all, when you purchase something, you're willing to pay an amount equal to your desire to own the product, so the better you position your product's relevance to your potential client's needs, the more price becomes irrelevant. However, the selling climate has changed so dramatically in the past several years that price has become more of a legitimate, stand-alone objection, an objection many salespeople still have a tough time overcoming. As I wrote about in "Hard Times, Part 1," the problem has intensified over the last few years because price (instead of product value) too often becomes the major issue. Where we used to regroup, reevaluate and then reinforce the value of our product once we received a price objection, the tendency today is to drop trou and, more or less, beg for the business. We've educated the buyer too well, and she now knows she can get a better deal by simply asking for it. And because business is much more competitive and harder to come by, we feel pressured into accepting terms dictated by the client rather than risk losing a sale.

A sad state of affairs, for sure. And because of the inherent danger of panic discounting, we're now fighting an uphill battle against an obstacle of our own making, an obstacle where, in the long run, we could meet our Waterloo. It reminds me of a cartoon I once saw. The cartoon depicted a man in tattered clothing who looked like a hobo, unshaven, with the pockets of his pants turned inside-out and hanging by his side, indicating he was broke. He had a quizzical expression on his face with his arms outstretched and his hands open to the heavens.

The caption beneath the caricature read, "But I always put in the lowest bid!"

What may be expensive to one person might be cheap to another, depending on the perceived value each attaches to the product. If somebody offered you a new pickup truck for $1,000, that would be a great deal and very desirable, but if they offered you that same truck for $200,000, that would be preposterous and a bad deal. The cost of the product has to match the expectations of what the product's value will provide. There's an old joke that's been going around for as long as I can remember. This guy goes into a bar and is approached by a lady of the evening who sits down beside him and smiles. She leans in and whispers, "This is your lucky night. I will do anything you want for $400 if you can say it in three words." The guy reaches into his pocket and lays out four 100 dollar bills on the bar. He smiles back at her and says, "Paint my house."

A $400 tryst would probably be expensive and undesirable to most people, but getting your house painted for $400 would be a spectacular bargain. Of course, your house might end up looking a little screwy and you may be left with a blown opportunity, but that's to be expected from most bargains. In other words, you almost always get what you pay for.

Which is an important point to make to your prospect, and the best way to make that point is by holding firm on price, indicating your conviction of the product's value. I once heard of a fellow who worked for an advertising agency on Madison Avenue in New York City for 25 years. One day he decided he'd had enough of working for a big company and wanted to go out on his own, so he left the agency and opened his own advertising consulting business. After six months, he hadn't landed any clients and he was struggling mightily. One day he was having lunch with the CEO of his old agency, and he told his ex-boss the problems he was experiencing. The boss asked him how much he was charging and the fellow told him he was asking for $200 an hour. The boss told him to raise his price to $500 an hour. The fellow thought his old boss was nuts, but he was desperate to try anything, so he did it. Within no time at all, this delighted fellow was so busy he had to hire an associate to help handle all the business, and he ended up becoming one of the most successful advertising consulting firms in the city.

Believe it or not, price is one of the surest ways to establish value. If you pitch your product professionally and present your price forthrightly with no apologies or equivocation, prospects will get the message that your product has real value. Remember, price is merely as important as you allow it to be. The only significance it holds in the selling process is comparable to perceived needs or desires. If a prospect needs or wants your product, price simply becomes a perfunctory detail. So it's imperative to sell value first, which is not easy, if not impossible to do, if you haven't first built a foundation of trust, because it always comes down to a matter of trust.

If you're honest and allow yourself to care about the well-being of your clients, everything else will fall into place. Keep in mind you can only fake it for so long, and you'll only be truly successful if you believe in your product, and people will only buy from you if they believe you believe in them, too.

Trust. It's a beautiful thing.

Hook Me Up, Buttercup

Lean on me.

Or better yet, let me lean on you.

That's the basic (albeit somewhat cynical) principle of most networking groups. From chambers of commerce to business clubs to leads groups to the semi-secret, marginally mysterious fraternal orders of this or that, networking organizations have been around since the small but effective inaugural networking meeting where Adam introduced Eve to the Serpent who then proceeded to trade our immortal souls for a taste of knowledge. Talk about deficit spending!

Eve was the preliminary, primordial prospect, successfully networked by the world's first and foremost fork-tongued, slippery, slithering salesman. And here we are several millennia later (or thereabout, give or take a few million years, depending on your interpretation of the space-time continuum), still trying to use our fellow original-sinners to help us with introductions to ripe, juicy prospects.

I have used networking groups over the course of my career with mixed results, depending on the area, the group, my product and—most important—my commitment to making it work to my benefit.

But before we dig in, let's set a couple of ground rules.

Rule Number 1: Everybody's in sales. I know that must be depressing for many of you, but we're all out on the street soliciting, flashing our goods and plying our trade (figuratively speaking, of course). Even you doctors and lawyers who went to school to distance yourselves from the rumbling horde are up to your stethoscopes and *habeas corpora* selling your services, only with fancier degrees and more arcane products.

Rule Number 2: Those who are smart and industrious in selling their product or service will prevail while all others will fall behind. The world of doing business has changed, and if you don't change with it, you'll be left in the wake and end up swimming with the fishes.

Smart and industrious selling starts with smart and industrious prospecting. There are many ways to prospect and find new customers, but they basically fall into five categories, listed in ascending order:

5. cold calling,

4. networking,

3. referrals and recommendations,

2. existing and past customers, and

1. contacts through your rich and influential family.

Say you're deficient in category number one due to an unfortunate accident of birth, so your existing customers and your past customers represent your best opportunity for new business. Look, I've been around the block a time or two and I know most organizations take the position that renewal business is easy and grows on the money tree in the backyard. Don't fall for that neatly packaged sophistry. Repeat business can sometimes be harder to keep than new business is to develop. All billing you obtain is new business. Period.

Getting referrals and recommendations is where most salespeople fail miserably, and we all get night sweats over cold calling.

That leaves networking, which is a relatively painless and effective method for meeting new prospects, if done correctly. If done incorrectly, it can be a huge waste of time and money. I built my first business through contacts I made at the chamber of commerce, and a guy I used to work with made a lot of money using his contacts through his Freemasons Lodge. One of my neighbors built up a nice clientele from his involvement in the Lions Club, and I had a salesman working for me who developed 100 percent of our business in a medium-sized market through a paid membership in a leads club.

On the other hand, I've had salespeople who got nothing out of leads clubs, and I've been part of business groups that were too large or so diverse that they offered no real help in networking my business.

On top of all those choices of where to put your time and money, there's a proliferation of free business groups and leads clubs springing up all over the place; a sign of the times. However, like everything else, I have seen some good ones and some not so good ones.

So the trick is to find the right group for your product and your market, and that can be difficult and time consuming. Talk to local business leaders and get their opinions. Go online and read up on the different groups—their websites should give you a pretty good indication of their proficiency. Most groups will let you attend at least one meeting free, so take advantage of that and talk to as many members as you can. Get their business cards and call them; ask a lot of questions. Do your homework up front and it will pay off in the long haul.

However, it doesn't matter what group you join if you don't work the group. The key to success with any of these types of organizations is putting time and effort into getting to know the members individually. You'll have a chance to meet many of them at the meetings, but the real value comes from getting together one on one, an area where many people are less than diligent.

Like the guy who buys the most expensive smartphone, chock-full of neat bells and whistles, but ends up using only about 10 percent of its capabilities, if you don't work the group, you're just there for show, a collection of blinking lights and pretty graphics with no discernable use.

Scrambled Eggs

I had a big day planned. It was Monday and I got to the office early so I could hit the road by 8:30. I had appointments set for 9:00 and 10:15, and then planned to do some cold-calling to fill out the morning. It was a beautiful, late-summer day with a slight hint of autumn in the air and I was excited about my prospects. You know, *carpe diem* and all that other simplistic, motivational-speaker jibber-jabber. I'd been trying for months to get an appointment with the person I was seeing at 9:00; he was a legitimate prospect who could potentially spend a great deal of money.

When I arrived fifteen minutes early, I was told by the receptionist he was running about fifteen minutes late and to please have a seat. I sat there reading and stewing until 9:30 when I finally asked if she had heard anything yet. She smiled and said she hadn't, but it shouldn't be too much longer. Finally, at 9:45, I left.

Peeved to the max.

I got to my 10:15 early since it was only a ten-minute drive, which worked out fine because that appointment's assistant was in the process of calling me to let me know my meeting was cancelled. Apparently, some emergency with one of her kid's braces was the excuse *du jour*, and I was having none of it. The assistant was one of those disturbingly bubbly people who would irritate me on the best of days, and her joyfully beaming sweet talk was only exacerbating the situation.

She was so damned happy while I was so damned unhappy. My irritation and disappointment were thinly veiled and I probably wasn't very pleasant to the animated, Nicholsonesque joker from hell. I was in no mood to be nice—not on this morning, not the way it was going so far.

I drove down the street and came to a red light. Across the intersection was a giant beer store, and next to it was a diner. The beer store wasn't open yet, so I went into the diner and ordered breakfast. I ate my eggs and read the paper, and, as I was finishing, the waitress walked over and said, "There were two ladies sitting at that table," pointing across the room.

The next thing she said ripped a hole in my isolated universe of alienation and self-pity. "They paid for your breakfast."

"What! They paid for my breakfast?" I repeated, trying to sort out the conflicting freight trains of surprise and suspicion colliding in my head. "What do you mean they paid for my breakfast?"

"They asked for your check and paid it. That's all I know," the waitress offered in a calming tone, trying to help me through this unexpected experience.

"Who were they?" I asked, but the waitress had no idea.

"Maybe it was just a random act of kindness," she said, giving me a tender smile as she hurried away to resume her responsibilities.

I'm sure I would have recognized the women if I knew them. What did they want with me? Whatever they wanted, they sure weren't getting any since I had no idea who they were. Did I look like I needed a free meal, like I should be standing on an off-ramp with a sign reading "Will manifest a look of complete bewilderment for food"? I was having serious trouble wrapping my brain around this one. I understood being stood up for appointments and discourteous customers—I'd been dealing with that type of thoughtlessness for 35 years—but this was an altogether different animal.

Why was this happening to me? Why were they messing with my neat, little world? Who would subject me to such pain and torment?

I decided to confront the cashier. I would ask her if the women paid with a credit card, and if so, would she please give me the name on the card. I wasn't sure she would, but it was worth a chance to end this downright disturbing dilemma. As I waited in line while another customer paid his check, I caught a glimpse of myself in the mirror behind the cashier's stand. I looked demonic. My brow was furrowed and my eyes were narrowed in consternation; my lips were twisted in a look of barely suppressed anger. It was a frightening and shocking sight.

What was I thinking?

Somebody did something nice for me, for no discernable reason and with no apparent ulterior motive, and here I stood, ready to fight to the death, to annihilate and banish these seemingly kind, good Samaritans from the face of the earth. My wrath was palpable.

And wholly misplaced.

I got out of there quickly and sat in my car staring at a scantily clad Betty Boop dancing inside the fluid globe of the suicide knob attached to my steering wheel, thinking about what had just happened and trying to figure out what was going on with me. I'd let myself go to a very bad place, from my first disappointment of the morning until a generous gesture of gentle humanity brought out the resentment and guilt that resides in all our souls; in most of us it's kept safely under control in the dungeons of our deepest psyches, while in others is easily brought to the surface with the slightest provocation. And from whichever position you come, it's always your choice.

I thought I'd learned that lesson before, many times over, but some disciplines take constant vigilance and caution as *we few, we happy few* navigate the labyrinth of self-doubt and narcissistic pride on the precarious course of exchanging commodities or services for monetary consideration.

The profession of sales can be one bitch of a mistress!

"Driving in my car, smoking my cigar" (I don't really smoke but I love that Jack Bruce lyric), I couldn't turn it off; my mind kept coming back to how I'd let myself get "tangled up in blue" (a Dylan lyric I also happen to love and aren't we having a swell time playing *Name That Tune?*). I thought of Zig Ziglar and one of his legendary parables I'd recently been reintroduced to on YouTube.

The video is called *Attitude Makes All the Difference*, and I highly recommend watching it if for no other reason than to catch Ziglar at his animated and entertaining best. You may find Zig a wee bit old-fashioned (and if you don't, then you most likely didn't have to Google any of the references in the proceeding paragraphs), but his message is timeless and as valuable today as it was when he first set out peddling his homespun, salt-of-of-the-earth philosophy. I won't ruin it for you by retelling the story (I couldn't do it justice, anyway), but the message is that you have all the power to control how the world treats you.

Surprise, surprise. You're in charge. It all comes down to your attitude, like everything else, and that's not such a big surprise after all.

But "it don't come easy" (yes, another tattered and frayed lyric from days gone by, delivered by the least formidable of the most formidable, Richard Starkey, and have fun with that one on Google). You have to work at it and work at it every day. A good attitude does not magically appear with the wave of a wand and a puff of smoke, but comes from preparation and execution.

It's my hard-earned belief that success is not the result of a good attitude, but a good attitude is the result of success. And the only way to achieve success is to work hard and work smart. If you do that, you will be successful. It's that simple.

And just as simple, a good attitude will follow like night follows day.

You can take that to the bank.

And one more thing. Note to The Big Guy: Next time you're gracious enough to visit me with a random act of kindness, could you please give me a heads up. I was going to have the eggs Benedict that morning, but I didn't want to go the extra three bucks.

Thank you.

Epilogue

Congratulations!
Today is your day.
You're off to Great Places!
You're off and away!

Dr. Seuss
Oh, the Places You'll Go

I've been in sales a long time and I've been given more sales advice than I can remember, much of it from the best and brightest who ever pounded the pavement. But the most excellent advice I ever got was through my kids.

Years ago when I used to read to them, I particularly enjoyed Dr. Seuss books. One night I picked out a new book my mother had recently given them that I had never read before called *Oh, The Places*

You'll Go. By the time I got halfway through it, I realized this was no children's book. This was a message for all ages, especially those of us in the ranks of the small but confident group of the initiated souls of the forever shifting brotherhood of drummers, canvassers and knockers.

I was blown away. This was the perfect manual for a salesperson; everything in it was spot-on regarding the ups and downs, the pain and the glory, the good habits and the bad distractions we face daily as we sometimes cheerfully, other times painfully, keep on dancing in the jaws of the dragon.

Since that time, I have heard of other sales managers and trainers who use the book, and it's become quite popular as a graduation gift. I even came across a couple of learned theses on its interpretive and allegorical meaning from the absurd to the sublime.

"So, be your name Buxbaum or Bixby or Bray, or Mordecai Ali Van Allen O'Shea," I recommend you buy a copy of the book and keep it with you for all those times when "you can get all hung up in a prickle-ly perch," because "I'm sorry to say so but, sadly, it's true, that Bang-ups and Hang-ups can happen to you."

I still go back to the book on those occasions when I "come down from the Lurch with an unpleasant bump," and every time I do, it's like taking a big old slice of fresh, clean water pie.

My, oh my.

Richard Plinke

You have brains in your head.
You have feet in your shoes.
You can steer yourself
any direction you choose.

Acknowledgments

I don't enjoy "Acknowledgment" sections of books, and I bet you don't either. As a matter of fact, I'm surprised you're even reading this. Acknowledgments are boring and obligatory and usually a bit self-indulgent, like you just wrote the next *Absalom, Absalom!* and it's absolutely imperative the world knows what hands went into the divinely inspired creation of such a *magnum opus.*

I'd be much more interested in mentioning a few people who were not very helpful or inspiring. What's an antonym for acknowledgment?

De-acknowledgment?

Okay, then, I'd like to take this opportunity to de-acknowledge one individual who seriously affected my writing career and who is singularly deserving of a grand de-acknowledgment.

Tom Collins.

I kid you not, that was his name. Tom Collins, my short, dumpy, hyperactive eleventh-grade English teacher. He died not too long after

I was out of high school so I never had the opportunity to thank him in person for the major de-contribution he made to my life.

I guess this is my only chance.

We had an assignment to write a poem. I forget the specific requirements of the assignment, but I played football. I didn't write poetry. The assignment was drudgery, and so naturally, I put it off until the last possible moment. I remember starting it at the breakfast table the morning it was due, and finishing it on the bus on my way to school.

This is the finished product of that morning's duress:

The Sentinel

Like a sentry standing guard
Is the ancient cedar tree
High upon his lofty hill
Ever watching over me

Mute and stern upon his post
History passing at his feet
Faithful soldier of the past
Battle-scarred by wind and sleet

Tom Collins thought the poem was great, so great that there was no possible way I could have written it. When it was handed back to me, he had given me an A+ with a note saying, "I'm sure this poem is plagiarized. I've looked everywhere I can think of but can't find the source. I know you cheated and you know you cheated, so you'll just have to live with that."

My only conscious thoughts were that the stupid assignment was done, I got a good grade, and I had football practice to get to. In reality, Tom Collins was a motivating and entertaining teacher who actually contributed to my love of literature eventfully coming out of the closet (after I quit playing football, of course).

So here's to you, Mr. Tom Collins, heaven holds a special place for you, wo, wo, wo.

Now that that's off my chest, there are a few people I would like to thank for their help. Without being maudlin or predictable, first and foremost I'd like to thank my wife, Terry, who on more than one occasion has been awakened from a sound sleep, handed sheets of paper and a red pen and instructed, "Read this!"

I would also like to thank Brenda Lange, who has been my editor, advisor and part-time therapist for the past couple years and who not only has the talent and the insight to sort the wheat from the chaff, but the good sense to keep telling me I'm a great writer. Her guidance and support have been inestimable.

Marian Wolbers brought a great deal of expertise in the arcane and mysterious world of book publishing. I went to college in the 70s where we learned that traditional sentence structure, syntax and punctuation were anachronistic impediments, and were taught to write from an individually expressive platform. Ha! Try selling that to Marian.

Finally, I'd like to thank John Hayes, a friend since we were the Young Turks making our way through the minefields of corporate dysfunction. Apart from his love of the New York Giants, John is a man of great judgment and composure, and he has given me the greatest gift one person can give to another: Encouragement.